# MURDER & MAYHEM
## IN SHEFFIELD

# Murder & Mayhem in Sheffield

## GEOFFREY HOWSE

First published in Great Britain in 2012 by
**Wharncliffe Books**
*an imprint of*
**Pen and Sword Books Ltd**
**47 Church Street**
**Barnsley**
**South Yorkshire**
**S70 2AS**

© Geoffrey Howse 2012

ISBN: 978-1-84563-154-3

The right of Geoffrey Howse to be identified as the author
of this work has been asserted by him in accordance with
the Copyright, Designs and Patents Act 1988.

A CIP catalogue record for this book is available from the
British Library.

Typeset in 11/13pt Plantin by Concept, Huddersfield.

Printed and bound in England by CPI Group (UK) Ltd,
Croydon, CR0 4YY.

Pen & Sword Books Ltd incorporates the imprints of
Pen & Sword Aviation, Pen & Sword Family History,
Pen & Sword Maritime, Pen & Sword Military,
Pen & Sword Discovery, Wharncliffe Local History,
Wharncliffe True Crime, Wharncliffe Transport,
Pen & Sword Select, Pen & Sword Military Classics,
Leo Cooper, The Praetorian Press, Remember When,
Seaforth Publishing and Frontline Publishing.

For a complete list of Pen & Sword titles please contact
PEN & SWORD BOOKS LIMITED
47 Church Street
Barnsley
South Yorkshire
S70 2BR
England
E-mail: enquiries@pen-and-sword.co.uk
Website: www.pen-and-sword.co.uk

# Contents

This book is dedicated to the memory
of my aunt and uncle,
**Iris Ackroyd** (1925–2012)
and
**Jack Ackroyd** (1924–1980)

# Acknowledgements

Keith Atack, Vera Atack, Michael Barber, Susan Barber, Tony Briggs, Robert (Bob) A. Dale, Kathleen Dale, Iris J. Deller, Joanna C. Murray Deller, Ricky S. Deller, Tracy P. Deller, Brian Elliott, Ann Howse, Kristin J. Finney, Doreen Howse, Kathleen Howse, Dr Hidayat Hussein, Matt Jones, Heather Law, Kevin McGovern, Susan McGovern, Brenden E. McNally, Linne Matthews, Raymond Mellor-Jones, Pam Mott, Eleanor Nelder, Stanley Nelder, Anthony Richards, David J. Richardson, Rose Vickers, Adam R. Walker, Anna Walker, Arthur O. Walker, Christine Walker, Darren J. Walker, David Walker, Emma C. Walker, Ivan P. Walker, Jenny Walker, Paula L. Walker, Polly Walker, Suki B. Walker, Thomas Walker, Helen Weatherburn, Clifford Willoughby, Margaret Willoughby, the staff of Barnsley Central Library Local Studies Department, the Staff of Sheffield Central Library Local Studies Department, the staff of the British Library Newspaper Archive at Colindale.

Also thanks to John D. Murray, who has assisted me over many years. And finally, not forgetting my ever-faithful walking companion, Coco.

# Introduction

On this book I have attempted to give the reader an insight into some of the chaotic disturbances, acts of violence and dreadful murders that have been committed in Sheffield by Sheffielders and incomers, from the eighteenth century to the middle of the twentieth century, when, in 1947, the last Sheffielder to be judicially hanged committed murder. Many of the locations are still familiar to us in the present day; others are but distant memories, such as the site of the exotic sounding Sands Paviours, covered today by the City Hall, which opened in 1932.

In my efforts to bring these cases to the printed page I have delved through countless books, documents, newspapers and manuscripts, as well as drawing on the extensive research on the history of Sheffield I have undertaken over almost two decades. Some of the murder cases I have covered I have provided only the bare bones to the events surrounding what are, in some instances, fairly complex affairs. Other murders are dealt with in greater depth.

I apologise unreservedly for any errors or omissions.

# CHAPTER 1

# Sheffield's Broad Canvas for Murder and Mayhem

## *A band of young men numbering from 100 to 200, armed with sticks, brooms and rolls of bills torn off the walls, began parading the streets at a trot ...*

Sheffield has for centuries enjoyed an enviable world-wide reputation for the high quality manufacturing industries on which the city has developed. Its cutlery industry was first mentioned in Geoffrey Chaucer's (c.1340–1400) *The Canterbury Tales*, when, at the beginning of The Reeves Tale, Chaucer mentions 'A Sheffield thwitel [whittler] baar he in his hose'. Sheffield has remained the world leader in the cutlery industry and, from the late seventeenth century onwards, it also became the most famous area in the world for the production of high quality steel. As the area has evolved into the modern city we know today many changes have taken place. With few exceptions, the oldest buildings to survive intact in the city centre date from the early Georgian period, although many street names stand as reminders of Sheffield's medieval past.

Unfortunately, the finest examples of medieval buildings were situated around the site of Sheffield's ancient castle and their remains lie buried beneath the modern Castle Market. In other parts of Sheffield, large numbers of medieval buildings were torn down during the eighteenth, nineteenth and early twentieth centuries. Sheffield Castle itself, a once magnificent structure, had Norman origins. It was destroyed in 1649–50, when Parliament ordered that all castles that had been fortified by the Royalists during the Civil War should be demolished.

In *A Tour through the Whole Island of Great Britain* (1724–27), Daniel Defoe writes of Sheffield:

> The town of Sheffield is very populous and large, the streets narrow, and the houses dark and black, occasioned by the continued smoke of the forges, which are always at work.

In 1736, not long after Defoe's visit, the population was 10,121, with a further 4,410 living in the rural parts that comprised the extensive parish of Sheffield. When one compares the population of other towns and cities at that time, Sheffield would have indeed been considered large, as the entire population of England amounted to less than 6 million. London had, for the time, an enormous population of 500,000 but the next largest city, Norwich, had a population of around 30,000. So Sheffield, although still a town, and with an ever-increasing population, soon overtook many cities and county towns in size. Sheffield was at the centre of Hallamshire, a district within a district – being situated with Yorkshire's West Riding, yet contained within an enclave that for generations has been referred to as South Yorkshire. Hallamshire, a district of 72,000 acres, broadly speaking comprised the then parishes of Sheffield and Ecclesfield and the Chapelry of Bradfield. The parish of Sheffield was incorporated as the borough of Sheffield in 1843 and the town was granted City Charter in 1893. At the beginning of the twenty-first century, Sheffield has a population of more than 500,000.

The growth of Sheffield and its industrial expansion was largely due to its geographical location. Like Rome, Sheffield is built on seven hills. It was, however, not its hills that made Sheffield a great industrial centre but its water supply. Sheffield is blessed with five river valleys, the rivers being the Don, Loxley, Porter, Rivelin and Sheaf (the river from which the name Sheffield is derived). The plentiful supply of water, combined with the rich beds of iron ore and ample timber available locally, hastened the development of the iron and steel industries. Scores of dams were built in the river valleys to hold water to turn hundreds of water wheels. Timber was turned into charcoal for the smelting and forging industries, making Sheffield a great centre of industry long before the Industrial Revolution came along, after which coal became the main source of power for Sheffield's industries.

By the time of the first official census in 1801, the population of the parish of Sheffield had risen to 45,755, of whom 31,314 resided within the central township. Rapid expansion continued and fifty years later, the population numbered 135,310. The increase in population resulted in extensive building throughout Sheffield. In the centre, the changes to Sheffield's buildings have been more concentrated. The houses that once proliferated in central Sheffield during the eighteenth, nineteenth and early twentieth centuries have largely disappeared, as more and more people moved to the suburbs. Buildings have replaced buildings, sometimes several times over, and often they have left little trace of the thriving communities of Sheffielders that once lived and worked in the locality. Within the present-day streets there are, however, some reminders of the city's past.

It was during the reign of Queen Victoria that the foundations of the Sheffield we know today were laid. During that period a commercial quarter was created in the central area and the township was extended westwards, north-westwards and eastwards as new middle-class estates and working-class

*A view of Sheffield in the 1830s from the south-east.* (Author's collection)

suburbs were developed, far beyond the boundaries of the ancient township. In the eastern portion immigrants came from elsewhere in Yorkshire, some from Derbyshire and smaller numbers from Nottinghamshire, Leicestershire and various other English counties, and they soon filled the terraces that had been built to accommodate the new workforce. Some immigrants came from Ireland and settled mostly in the north-western quarter of central Sheffield. A few people came from Scotland, and even fewer from Wales. There were also some German immigrants during this period.

During the second half of the nineteenth century the steel industry surpassed cutlery making as the area's major industry. The need for high quality steel for railways, ship-building and armaments meant that the Sheffield steel barons no longer looked to the cutlery industry as their major customer. Although industry in Sheffield was booming, the downside was that the concentration of heavy industry resulted in the townscape changing dramatically and, some residents thought, unfavourably. Large numbers of Sheffielders connected with the cutlery industry emigrated, particularly to the United States of America, and they became employed in the cutlery industry there. Some returned but many former Sheffield families settled permanently overseas. During the second half of the twentieth century, industrial production methods changed and hundreds of acres of steelworks and factory buildings were demolished as they became surplus to requirements, as did the workforce. Thousands became unemployed. At first the recovery was slow but Sheffield remains a forward-thinking city and expansion has taken place in other areas, providing diverse forms of employment. Sheffield still remains the world leader in the cutlery and steel industries. Modern production methods mean that considerably fewer people work in these industries today, yet although the steel industry employs less than 10 per cent of the workforce it did in the early twentieth century, more tons of steel are currently being produced in Sheffield than at any time during its history. Today, Sheffield is England's fourth-largest city. It is also the greenest and is situated right at the centre of Britain. More than 9 million people live within an hour's drive of the city, and 20 million within two hours' drive.

The 1790s saw a period of considerable unrest in Sheffield. Following the Cutlers' Company losing its ancient right to regulate admissions into its trades in 1791, rioting and, on occasions, mob rule became the order of the day for some contingents in various communities within Sheffield. That same year, rioters were able to stall the enclosure of Crookes Moor until, on 27 July, a company of Light Dragoons arrived from Nottingham. A large crowd of sightseers gathered in the town centre to welcome their arrival. Within hours the sightseers had expanded or virtually been replaced by a mob that had swelled to several hundreds. They immediately singled out the nearest symbol of local authority to attack, the town gaol, in King Street. They broke down its doors, shattered the windows and freed the prisoners. Then the shout went up: 'To Broom Hall', the residence of the town's chief magistrate, the Reverend James Wilkinson, who had been responsible for obtaining an Act of Enclosure for Crookes Moor and other areas of waste and common land amounting to 6,000 acres. On arrival at Broom Hall they proceeded to break all the windows, destroy some of the furnishings, damage or burn Reverend Wilkinson's library and set fire to his haystacks. The mob dispersed when the Dragoons arrived, and back in the town centre broke the windows at the house of the Duke of Norfolk's Agent, Vincent Eyre. Other acts of violence were perpetrated and rule was only restored the following day after the arrival of reinforcements from York. Five rioters were arrested and committed to York Assizes. Four were eventually released, but one, eighteen-year-old apprentice John Bennett, was found guilty of rioting and arson and was hanged on Saturday, 6 September. In consequence of this rioting, Sheffield was granted its own garrison. Work began in July 1792 at a site at Philadelphia, beyond Shalesmoor, and when completed held 200 officers and men. These buildings were replaced in 1849 by Hillsborough Barracks.

Like many of England's manufacturing towns that were either inadequately or not at all represented by a parliamentary seat, several reformers and some agitators were active in Sheffield. Disappointment followed the Reform Act of 1832 and a new campaign for parliamentary reform focussed on six points of a charter of demands. The movement for these reforms became known as Chartism, and its followers as Chartists. The more sober-minded operating within Sheffield, such as Ebenezer Elliott and Isaac Ironside, advocated 'moral force' as a means of achieving their aims but there were other factions who saw 'physical force' as the way forward. These uglier factions of Sheffield's would-be reformers comprised a few well-meaning but probably disillusioned individuals, swelled by a contingent of men who were little more than thugs, many of them being in it for the fight but couldn't care less about the cause. Clandestine meetings were held by torch-light and plots were hatched. Then, in January 1840, Samuel Holberry, an ex-soldier who was Nottinghamshire born and raised but by then resident in Sheffield, plotted to lead an uprising in which he planned to seize the Town Hall and the Tontine Inn, murder the watchmen and set fire to the houses of magistrates and many other prominent Sheffield citizens. The plot was betrayed and, in March, Holberry and seven others involved in the plot were tried at York for 'seditious conspiracy'.

*Sheffield's old Town Hall, Waingate, photographed by Keith Atack in the present day. Sheffield's first town hall stood in the south-east corner of St Peter's churchyard and opened in 1700, with make-do court facilities and three cells. The Town Hall seen here that replaced it opened in 1808. Its distinctive tower was added in 1866. The building provided court facilities from its opening until the 1990s.* (Author's collection)

*The Tontine Hotel, depicted here in 1830. Sometimes known as the Tontine Inn, along with the Town Hall, seen in the previous image, they were the intended targets for the failed uprising planned by Samuel Holberry and his associates, in 1840.* (Author's collection)

All were found guilty. Holberry was given the longest sentence – four years in Northallerton House of Correction. There he was badly treated and his health deteriorated until, in September 1841, he was moved to York Castle. Suffering from consumption, he was moved to a hospital ward and died in June 1842. He was twenty-seven years old. Holberry was buried in Sheffield General Cemetery. Thousands lined the streets to watch his funeral cortège pass by.

The Sheffield Outrages, as a series of incidents that occurred in the late 1850s and 1860s became known, were the result of Sheffield's success in cutlery production and heavy industry. Many of those involved in the steel industries were obliged to work long shifts in often desperately unpleasant conditions. Industrial disease was rife and one particular disease, known as 'Grinders' Asthma', was suffered by many workers in Sheffield's cutlery industry. Perhaps unsurprisingly, Sheffield became one of the main centres for agitation and trade union organization, and industrial unrest culminated in a small group of militants carrying out these outrages, which involved attacking ordinary working men for non compliance and physical attacks on employers, culminating in a series of explosions and even murder.

A practice known as 'rattening', by which a grinder who had fallen foul of his workmates might be disciplined, had been common practice for a considerable time before these outrages took place. Rattening involved the removing or destroying of bands connecting the grindstone with the revolving shaft, making it completely inoperable. Rattening increased during these outrages, as did violent attacks. These incidents included the murder of saw grinder James Linley, in 1859, and an explosion in a house in Acorn Street, which caused the death of a female lodger. The outrages continued, resulting in the Government deciding to hold a Royal Commission on the trade unions and an inquiry into the Sheffield Outrages.

The findings of the commission showed that of the sixty trade unions in Sheffield, twelve had resorted to outrage. Over a ten-year period they had gathered information concerning 166 rattenings, and twenty serious outrages, in addition to cases of intimidation and twenty-two threatening letters. The most violent of the unions had been the Saw Grinders' Society. The outrages came to an end but rattening continued after the Royal Commission's findings had been published, and over the following twenty years, fifty-six cases were reported, a third involving saw grinders.

On Wednesday, 18 November 1868, the *Sheffield and Rotherham Independent* reported:

> The members for Sheffield in the new Parliament are Mr Hadfield re-elected, Mr Mundella elected vice and Mr Roebuck, ignominiously defeated yesterday.
>
> The day was a regular November day, dull and drizzling, but the heaviness of the weather was by no means reflected in the spirits of the townsfolk. Eight o'clock saw hundreds upon hundreds of men eagerly wending their way to the various polling places, with the gravity of men on a serious and solemn business. The arrangements at some of the polling booths were as bad as they could possibly be, men being kept half and three quarters of an hour before they could record their votes. In one place a crowd was jammed

for half an hour into a passage 12ft long, with two policemen at the further end to prevent their admission into a
spacious room, except one at a time every three or four
minutes. All this, however, was patiently borne, and the
inconvenience to which the voters were put only found
utterances in a few mild jokes ... In the centre parts of town
business proceeded as usual for an hour or two, but about
eleven o'clock the gathering crowds in the area and the
growing excitement caused the more timid, or the more
prudent shopkeepers to put up their shutters ... Towards
twelve o'clock a wild and semi-criminal element began to
show itself. A band of young men numbering from 100 to
200, armed with sticks, brooms and rolls of bills torn off the
walls, began parading the streets at a trot. After they had
carried on this game for some time, they gained courage to
rob, and broke into a shop in Paradise Street, to steal cigars,
and into the shops in Sheffield Moor, and other places.
Their numbers grew from time to time, and the rapid
closing of the shops showed that danger was expected ...
The stock of fish in the shop of Mr Langley, Gibraltar
Street, was promptly confiscated, and the fish were stuck
on sticks and poles and carried off in triumph ... This
enterprising band of ragamuffins proceeded up Scotland
Street, where they soon attacked another fish shop ... The
mob then moved off to a fruiterer's shop across the way,
and soon apples and nuts were rolling by scores down the
street ... As the time drew on for the closing of the poll,
excited crowds thronged the central streets, and he who got
100 yards without losing his hat had reason to believe
himself born under a lucky star ... The gang were not
content with simply smashing windows, but in one or two
instances they made free with the contents of the shops ...

On Saturday, 19 December, three Sheffield men appeared
before Mr Justice Brett at Leeds Assizes in connection with
offences committed during the election riots in Sheffield the previous month. Thomas Moore, aged twenty-eight, blade striker,
Robert Morton, aged twenty-one, cutler, and Norman Hall,
aged forty-one, blade forger, were indicted for 'feloniously and
violently assaulting with sticks and bludgeons John Smith and

stealing from his person a gold-plated Albert watchguard; also stealing from the dwelling house of the said John Smith the sum of £5 in money; and also putting him in bodily fear by reason of threats and menaces, at Sheffield on 17 November.' Mr Barker prosecuted and Mr Blackburn defended. The jury found all three prisoners guilty and Mr Justice Brett sentenced all three men to twelve months' imprisonment.

At the same hearing, Edward Gillet, a twenty-one-year-old spring knife grinder, was also found guilty of stealing property during the election riots on 17 November. He was sent to prison for six months for breaking into the shop of James Towler, with several other unidentified men, and stealing, amongst other sundry items, 3 pounds in weight of cigars.

Gambling gangs had featured in Sheffield since the early years of the twentieth century but they flourished during the First World War, when miners and steelworkers passed a leisurely hour or two after their shifts aiding the war effort and handing over their hard-earned cash to those controlling the proceedings, who turned in a healthy profit. During the 1920s, when the post-war slump had reduced the pool of gamblers considerably, various rival gangs decided they wanted a bigger piece of the action.

Sheffield's gambling gangs made nationwide news through a series of incidents that became known as the Sheffield Gang Wars. The wars came about over who should have control of the lucrative tossing rings on Sky Edge. The Skyring, or Sky Edge Gambling Ring, as it was sometimes known, involved the game of pitch and toss – an elaborate form of heads or tails, on which men would place bets, sometimes gathering in their hundreds underneath Norfolk Bridge. This ring was controlled by George Mooney and the Mooney Gang, of West Bar. After Mooney decided he wanted a bigger share of the action for himself, he thinned out the gang's membership and this resulted in a rival gang being formed, which became known as the Park Brigade, who followed Sam Garvin, from the Park area. This rivalry continued between 1923–25, with a whole range of unpleasant incidents occurring and various gang members being slashed with razors. It culminated in murder, in April 1925, when some of Sam Garvin's men attacked a Scotsman named Plommer, in Princess Street, Attercliffe (see Chapter 4). It was the Special Duties Squad, instigated by Lieutenant Colonel Hall-Dallwood, the chief constable, who retired in March 1926, and his successor, Captain Percy J. Sillitoe (later head of MI5), that finally busted the by then infamous Sheffield gangs.

# CHAPTER 2

# Murders in Sheffield from 1782 to 1800

*Following his conviction for murder, he was visited by his wife in the condemned cell. He contritely told her that, had he listened to her, he would not have ended up as he had ...*

### Frank Fearne, 1782

The son of a Bradfield farmer, eighteen-year-old Frank Fearne was apprenticed to a Sheffield filesmith. Many people in the town who knew him regarded him as an idle waster. Early in 1782, he called in at the High Street shop of watchmaker Nathan Andrews. A watch club had recently started up in Bradfield, and Fearne offered to introduce Andrews to the members and put some business his way. Andrews said he would pay them a visit but only when the membership had reached twenty, so Fearne bided his time.

A while later, Fearne called in on Andrews again and informed him that the membership now exceeded all his expectations and arranged to take him to Bradfield, along with sample watches to show the members. Fearne had a half-day holiday due from work so he arranged to meet Andrews on the afternoon of Thursday, 18 March and the two men set out for Bradfield. What the unfortunate Mr Andrews did not know was that Fearne had both a knife and a pistol secreted on his person.

It was around 4.00 pm when they reached Kirk Edge that they passed a young man named Wood, who was on his way to work in some nearby fields. He knew Fearne and they greeted one another with the usual pleasantries and Wood carried on his way and was soon out of sight. At this point Fearne lagged behind Andrews, pulled a pistol from his pocket and shot him in the back. Fearne then stabbed Andrews with the knife and

*Bradfield, where Sheffield watchmaker Nathan Andrews was heading when he was lured to his death by Frank Fearne.* (Author's collection)

smashed his skull with a hedge stake. Fearne then took to his heels, making off with Andrews' sample watches.

At dusk, Wood came upon Andrews' body on his way home from work. He fetched help and the body was carried to the workhouse. At that point Wood had no idea who the person was but on seeing the body in a lighted room, he quickly realized it was the very man he had seen with Fearne earlier that afternoon. Back in the town, Mr Andrews' failure to return had been noted and when it became known that a man had been found murdered at Kirk Edge, the body was swiftly identified as being that of the unfortunate watchmaker.

Fearne was quickly singled out as the prime suspect and the following night, a constable paid a visit to his lodgings in

Hawley Croft. Fearne was in bed. Having been roused from his slumbers, he was told by the constable that he was suspected of being involved in the murder of Nathan Andrews. Fearne denied any knowledge of it but when his room was searched several watches belonging to Andrews were found. Fearne was arrested and taken to the Town Hall cells. He was subsequently committed to trial at the Summer Assizes, where he was tried before Mr Justice Eyre. Frank Fearne was executed at York Tyburn on Tuesday, 23 July 1782, and was afterwards gibbeted on Loxley Common, where the body remained until, on Christmas Day 1797, Fearne's skeleton fell from the cage of the gibbet.

### James Beaumont, 1796

Estranged from his wife and children, filesmith James Beaumont lived with Sarah Turton in a house in the Nursery district of Sheffield. (Located near The Wicker, it was where the Duke of Norfolk kept his nursery.) On the night of Monday, 9 May 1796, he strangled Sarah Turton and, resolving to kill his wife, made his way round to a shop in Barley-field, which his wife kept, and attempted to gain admittance. Alarmed by her husband's appearance, and fearing something was seriously amiss, she refused to let him in. It was not long before Beaumont was arrested and soon afterwards was committed to York for trial, which took place in the Summer Assizes, before Mr Justice Lawrence. Following his conviction for murder, he was visited by his wife in the condemned cell. He contritely told her that, had he listened to her, he would not have ended up as he had. Beaumont was executed at York Tyburn on Monday, 18 July 1796, after which his body was given for dissection.

### Mary Thorpe, 1799

Described as being a respectable-looking girl in contemporary accounts, in September 1799, the unmarried Mary Thorpe left her home in Ecclesfield for Sheffield, where she took lodgings with a widow named Hartley. She gave a false name, calling herself Ashford. Mary was heavy with child, reputedly having been made pregnant, as she was later to remark, by a gentleman 'far above her in circumstances who had taken advantage of that elevation to tempt her on to her destruction.' In November, Mary gave birth to a boy. A week later, she left her lodgings, telling her landlady she was going to stay in Derby with her sister. Instead, she returned to Ecclesfield, although it seems not before breaking her journey to dispose of the relatively new addition to her life.

The morning following Mary's departure from Mrs Hartley's, the body of a baby boy was found in the river Don at Bridge Houses (near The Wicker). The fact that the child had been murdered was immediately evident. The little body was discovered wrapped in a cloth. Tied round the baby's neck was a tape weighted with a heavy stone. The tape was wrapped around the neck and tightly knotted no fewer than three times. The surgeon who examined the body confirmed that the baby had been strangled. The dead child had a distinctive birthmark. When word got around concerning the discovery of the body, Mrs Hartley came forward and a quick identification of the child was established.

Many of Mary's friends knew that she had been pregnant when she left Ecclesfield in September, and it did not escape their notice that she had clearly given birth before her return. She repeatedly denied that she had given birth and went as far as to say that they were mistaken, as she hadn't even been pregnant. This threw suspicion in her direction, as her friends knew otherwise. Quickly linked to the discovery of the dead child at Bridge Houses, she was tracked down and arrested by the parish constable at her father's house. On 27 November, an inquest was held before Coroner John Foster. The jury brought in a verdict of murder against Mary Thorpe. The coroner committed her for trial at the next assizes. She appeared before Mr Justice Rook on 14 March 1800, and, despite her managing to elicit a good deal of sympathy from the spectators, the jury convicted her. Mary Thorpe was hanged at York Tyburn on Monday, 17 March 1800. Afterwards, her body was given for dissection.

# CHAPTER 3

# Murders in Sheffield during the Nineteenth Century

## *The law is more humane to you than you were to your unhappy victim ...*

### William King, 1817

In 1817, thirty-year-old edge tool maker William King was cohabiting in Arundel Place with Sarah Trippet and their children, a three-month-old baby and a four-year-old boy. Sometime around six o'clock on the morning of 4 June, King was spotted by a neighbour pacing up and down the pavement in an agitated manner, outside his place of work in Furnival Street. When the neighbour called out, 'How are you?' he received the reply, 'I am but poorly, John.'

About half an hour later, the neighbourhood was awakened by the screams of a woman, which were followed by the sound of blows and loud groaning. The commotion, which had been quickly identified has having originated from William King's house, had brought out several neighbours into the street. One of them, George Woodcock, who lived two doors away, was moved to take swift action after it became apparent that the door was locked and someone noticed blood running down the glass panes of a first-floor bedroom window. The door having been broken open, Woodcock rushed up the stairs. There in the bedroom he found King standing by the bed with a blood-smeared poker in his hand. On the bed, with frightful injuries, lay the body of Sarah Trippet, with one of the children lying near its mother's bloodied head. Astounded and appalled at the incredulous scene he had been confronted with, Mr Woodcock blurted out, 'Good God! What is the matter? What have you done?'

King made no answer. He only responded by going for George Woodcock with the poker. Woodcock ran down the stairs and out of the house. He told the people outside what had occurred and asked them to guard the exit while he fetched a policeman.

Shortly, the fearful cries of a child could be heard, and another neighbour, John Goodland, made to enter the house as he called out to the other onlookers, 'Good God, he is murdering his children. Will nobody follow me up the stairs to prevent him?'

Nobody could summon up the courage to make the effort, so Goodland disappeared from the scene. Many people began to holler for King to come down. Within a few minutes he had done so, and as he emerged through the open doorway he backed against a wall with the poker held in his raised hand. While this was happening, John Goodland returned armed and quickly knocked the poker from King's hand. He and another neighbour then overpowered King and detained him until a constable arrived a short while later.

The constable asked King, 'What have you being doing?'

To which King replied, 'I've murdered my wife and children.'

Constable: 'For what cause?'

King: 'Jealousy. I did it with a poker and, if the deed were to do it again, I would do it.'

Constable: 'Have you been drinking?'

King: 'I was in the Swan with Two Necks last night and came home at ten o'clock.'

While this conversation was taking place, neighbours John Young and Mrs Halley went into the house and up to the bedroom. The baby was lying near its mother, the four-year-old boy sitting upright by her blood-soaked head. Mr Young detected signs of life and sped downstairs to get help but Sarah Trippet expired before medical help arrived.

William King was tried at the Summer Assizes, before Baron Wood. During the trial it emerged that King had met Sarah Trippet five years previously. She was married to a soldier serving under the Duke of Wellington. She struck up a friendship with King but before agreeing to live with him wrote to her husband's regiment concerning his whereabouts and received a reply telling her he had been killed. Sarah and King did not marry, despite her having borne him two children. Shortly before the murder, King discovered that Sarah's husband was still alive. Unfortunately, another soldier bearing the same name had been mistaken for Sarah's husband. Although witnesses unanimously agreed that he was a man given to drinking and sometimes flew into rages, King was undefended. The Crown's case being completed, when King was asked for his defence, his only reply was, 'I have nothing to say.'

Such was the weight of evidence against the prisoner that the jury returned a guilty verdict without having left the jury box to deliberate. Addressing King, Baron Wood said:

> After a long and patient investigation you have been found guilty by a jury of your country of the crime of murder. The crime is ... the most horrid that can be committed by a criminal or punished by the law; but in your case it was accompanied by circumstances of peculiar atrocity. The woman whom you have most clearly destroyed was a person with whom you cohabited and to whom you ought to have afforded protection. Instead of this, you not only murdered her but seemed to exult in the deed and to carry your malice even beyond death. The act which made everyone shudder produced no impression on you but a desire to renew it. Pray, therefore to God, during the short period you have to live that he may extend mercy to you in another world which you refused to one whom you ought to have protected in this.

His Lordship having then passed sentence of death, the prisoner was taken to the condemned cell to await his fate. William King became the first Sheffield murderer to be hanged at the New Drop, York. His execution took place on Thursday, 31 July 1817, and afterwards his body was given for dissection.

### James Mosley, 1821

On the afternoon of Friday, 3 August 1881, some grinders were enjoying a drink at a public house in Broad Street, Sheffield Park. Drinking in another room at The Harrow was a thirty-one-year-old table knife cutler named James Mosley. After several hours' drinking, one of the grinders, named Beuley, fancied a Banbury cake, but James Mosley was in the act of purchasing the last one. As Beuley tried to snatch it, a scuffle ensued. The men were separated and eventually Mosley left the premises, went to his brother-in-law's butcher's shop, where he purloined a knife, then went back to wait outside The Harrow, where he loitered by the entrance with the knife secreted under his smock frock. As the group of grinders left The Harrow half an hour or so later, Mosley lunged at Beuley with the knife, missed him and wounded his companion, James Mackay. Mackay was taken to the Sheffield Infirmary, where he died a month later, on 3 September, as a result of the injury received at the hand of James Mosley. Mosley was tried at York for murder on 16 March 1822. He was hanged on Saturday, 6 April.

## Martin Slack, 1828

In 1825, fifteen-year-old apprentice brace and bit maker Martin Slack lived in Norfolk Lane with his parents, five sisters and a brother. His sweetheart, Elizabeth Haigh, lived with her parents in North Street, West Bar. In 1828, Elizabeth became pregnant. The parish overseers were keen to ensure that the child would not become a burden on the poor rate and legal proceedings were taken against Slack, Elizabeth having named him on oath as the father. Elizabeth was still underage and her parents refused to give their consent for her to marry Slack. She gave birth to a baby girl on 19 October. Slack was ordered to pay a weekly sum for the child's maintenance, which he resented. On the evening of Saturday, 1 November, Slack visited Elizabeth and the baby and stayed until ten o'clock. He paid another visit early on Sunday morning at around seven o'clock. Elizabeth laid the baby on a settee and went upstairs to dress, leaving Slack in the same room as the child. Shortly afterwards she heard the baby's screams and came downstairs. Slack was sitting in a chair with the child in his arms. She took it from him and noticed smoke was coming from its mouth and what appeared to be brimstone on its lips. During her attempts to comfort her distressed baby she got some of the liquid on her own cheek and arm. It burnt her. She asked Slack if he had given the baby anything but he denied having done so and said it was just sick and to give the baby some water. When a surgeon was sent for he noticed a smell of *aqua fortis* (nitric acid). The baby died later that morning. Slack was tried at York Spring Assizes, before Baron Hullock. He strongly protested his innocence. Found guilty of murder, Martin Slack was hanged on Monday, 30 March 1829. He was eighteen years old. Afterwards, his body was given for dissection.

### William Allott, 1834

In 1834, Martha Hardwick owned a small dairy farm at Upper Heeley. William Allott, her cohabitee, and twelve-year-old milk boy Joseph Wolstenholme were the only residents. Allott styled himself farmer manager, and by all accounts was a domineering man who beat Martha whenever the fancy took him, often when he had taken strong drink, which he was prone to. On the morning of Tuesday, 9 September, Allott set off for Sheffield Town Hall to take a warrant out against his sister, claiming she had taken a sovereign from his box locker. The milk boy drove him there on the cart. Having conducted his business there, he immediately adjourned to an adjacent public house. At 3.00 pm Joseph Wolstenholme called in to say he was setting off home again. Allott still had a thirst for drink and declined to leave so the boy set off for the farm alone. He arrived there about 4.00 pm, fetched the cows from the field and, after they had been milked, chatted briefly with Martha before setting out again for Sheffield with the next delivery. He returned at 7.00 pm and unloaded the milk barrels. He told Martha he was going to take the cows up the fields and, having done so and his duties being finished, went off to play in the fields near the Waggon and Horses. Meanwhile, Allott had made his way back on foot and at 7.30 pm was in Sleigh Bush's grocer's shop in Bramall Lane. He met up with a neighbour, Joseph Cartwright, and they continued the short journey homewards together. Others they met on the journey home note how inebriated Allott was.

Later that evening, file forger George Rainey, who lived 30 yards from Martha Hardwick's farmhouse, heard a scream. He opened his door but on hearing nothing more he went back inside. Within minutes he heard another scream and went to the side of his workshop, where he could get a clear view of the farmhouse. He heard Allott's voice. He was cursing and swearing. He then heard Martha pleading with him, 'What have I done amiss, William?'

Shortly afterwards, young Joseph returned from playing in the fields and noticed blood on the kitchen floor. On going into the parlour he found Allott, his clothes all bloodied, lifting Martha onto the bed. Allott asked the boy, 'What hast thou been doing to get our mistress knocked on the head?'

Joseph replied, 'She was well and hearty when I took the cows to the field.'

Allott asked, 'How long have you been gone?'

Joseph replied, 'About half an hour.'

Allott then said, 'As I was walking up the field two men ran from the house. I tried to jump over a wall to cut them off but pulled my shoe to pieces doing so.'

However, Joseph was sharp enough to notice that as well as being torn, Allott's shoes had blood and hair on them. Martha Hardwick was a very sorry sight. Covered with blood, her hair was ruffled, her cap had been ripped off and the clothes torn from her back. She was in a delirious state and could not get up. As she was wiping blood off her face she called out, 'Help me! Come here!'

Allott carried on with the ruse that someone else was responsible for her injuries and it appears by then Martha was in no fit state to contradict him. But Allott's play acting belied the facts of what had been seen and heard by George Rainey and other neighbours. Medical attention proved unequal to her injuries and Martha died at ten o'clock. Allott was subsequently arrested and charged with murder. Allot was tried at the York Spring Assizes, in March 1835, before Baron Alderson. The jury convicted him of murder without retiring from the jury box. He was hanged on Monday, 6 April 1835. Afterwards, his body was buried within the castle precincts.

## Thomas Williams, 1837

Twenty-nine-year-old Thomas Williams was taken on as a basket maker in January 1837 by George Moore, the owner of a small factory in Silver Street Head, Sheffield. It soon became apparent to Mr Moore that his new employee was a heavy drinker and his work record was less than satisfactory, Williams often taking days off, preferring drinking to working. After several weeks, Mr Moore lost patience and at the beginning of March gave Williams two weeks' notice and took on Thomas

Froggatt to replace him. Subsequently, Mr Moore changed his mind and decided to keep both men on. However, Williams held a grudge against Froggatt, being of the opinion that he had tried to steal his job. The grudge shortly turned into absolute hatred.

On Friday, 17 March, Williams did not turn up for work and, having spent the morning drinking, went to Fargate and called at the lodgings of a basket maker called Buggins. The two of them went to the Black Swan for a drink. After ordering ale, Williams sat down with Buggins, telling him, 'I have a point of view and, if I can accomplish it, I will make you a present of my shears as I shall never use them again. You must keep them for my sake.'

On being pressed for an explanation Williams told Buggins of his intention to kill Froggatt and said he would mash his brains out that very night. The two men continued their drinking at another public house, Linley's, situated close to George Moore's factory. Williams went across to the factory during the course of the drinking session on two occasions; the second time he returned to Linley's, he announced to the assembled company, 'I've done it.'

When Buggins asked, 'What have you done?' Williams replied, 'I've killed old Frog.'

Buggins immediately went over to the factory, where he found Thomas Froggatt lying insensible on the workshop floor, with blood seeping out from two large wounds in his head. There was a billhook covered in blood on the floor nearby. As Thomas Froggatt was being taken to the hospital, Williams was setting off to take more drink in the Windsor Castle. It was there that Constable Waterfall went to arrest him. Williams told the constable, 'If he dies, I'll be satisfied. If not, I'll be sorry.'

Thomas Froggatt died of his injuries on 5 April. In due course, Thomas Williams was committed to trial at the Summer Assizes, before Mr Justice Coltman. Although his counsel, Mr Bliss, attempted to persuade the jury that his client was suffering from insanity 'irritated by drink', witness evidence persuaded them otherwise and they found him guilty of murder. Thomas Williams was hanged at noon on Saturday, 12 August 1837. He left a widow and five children. After praying on the scaffold, he had addressed the crowd:

Fellow men, you are come to witness a spectacle of intemperance, an awful scene; I hope this will make a lasting impression upon every soul before me. A man in the prime of his life, thirty years of age, cut off through this diabolical crime of intemperance. Is there a drunkard before me? Yes, I see many. Let him go home and be so no more. Is there a liar? Let him speak the truth for the future and turn to God with a full purpose of heart. I have to inform you that I am leaving a grateful partner behind me, one that is walking in the commandments of the Lord and one that delights in her God; therefore I hope I shall meet her in heaven. I have also not a doubt of my acceptance with that God whom I am going to stand before. Oh! That every one of you may seek the Lord because He may be found. May you turn to him and God Almighty grant that I may meet you all in the Kingdom of Heaven.

The bolt was drawn and Williams plummeted to his death, which came after a short struggle.

### Robert Nall, 1841

Robert and Mary Nall had married in 1833. It was not a successful union; the marriage had proved to be unsuccessful from the start. So much so that, during the eight years that followed, they had separated on no fewer than seven occasions. In January 1841 they parted again. By October, Nall wanted his wife back and during the course of the month turned up at Mary's mother's house, where she was lodging. Mary had had enough. Robert, however, was so persistent that it became necessary for Mary to take a summons out against him. After an unsuccessful attempt to see his wife in the early hours of Sunday, 27 October, Robert Nall turned up again at 9.00 am. This time he was successful. However, Mary said to him, 'I don't want to see you.'

Robert Nall: 'I am going out of town. Will you foot a pair of stockings for me?'

Mary Nall: 'No. Go and do the best for thyself.'

Robert Nall: 'Then I mean to tell thee what I mean to do. Thou must prepare thyself for a coffin tomorrow morning for I mean to stick thee.'

Later, Nall bumped into his sister-in-law, Ann Hal, in the street. She told him she wished he wouldn't behave so badly and that Mary had told her about preparing for a coffin. He told Ann that it was all nonsense, but on 3 November, he turned up at her house at Bridge Houses and told her to inform Mary that he was going to do what he had threatened. Despite this, he and Mary became reconciled and were back together again towards the end of the month. On the evening of 27 November, the couple turned up at the house of Lucy, Robert Nall's sister, in Bee Hive Lane, off Glossop Road, and asked for a bed for the night. Both were inebriated, but Robert was in a far worse state than his wife. Lucy provided them with accommodation and at 8.45 pm went out to visit a friend in Carver Street. When she returned about midnight she found her brother standing in front of the fire. When Lucy asked where Mary was, Robert replied he had been ill-using her and he thought he had killed her.

When Mary Nall's body was examined it was discovered that there were five wounds of a superficial nature to the neck, hand and shoulder, but the mortal wound was under the left breast. This extended to almost 4 inches deep and had passed through the liver, penetrating the stomach. An inquest was held at the Bee Hive public house on 30 November, at which the coroner told Nall he never knew a more deliberate and wicked act of murder.

Nall was tried at the Spring Assizes, before Mr Justice Coltman. After hearing the evidence the jury retired and returned after half an hour and pronounced the prisoner guilty but with a recommendation for mercy. Having placed the black cap on his head Mr Justice Coltman addressed Nall:

Robert Nall, you have been convicted of the crime of wilful murder; and though the counsel addressing the jury in your favour endeavoured to impress upon the jury the belief that you were not at the time you committed this act altogether a reasonable man, I found it my duty to tell the jury and I feel it my duty to tell you now that the state of mind you were in was not such as legally to extenuate your crime. You were responsible for your acts and in the interests of society you must suffer for it. Whether or not there may be in a moral point of view circumstances to extenuate, if not to justify, your conduct is a matter beyond my power or province to determine and I should be acting in a manner not so much as the country has a right to demand from me, if I did not tell you, in spite of the recommendation of the jury, that I see nothing whatever to justify me in holding out any prospect whatever that the sentence of the law will not be carried into effect. And with these remarks, entreating you to employ in the most profitable manner the short space of time that remains to you I have now to pronounce upon you the sentence of the law, which is that you are taken hence to the prison from whence you came and thence to a place of execution; that you there be hanged by the neck till your body be dead and that your body then be buried within the precincts of the prison in which you shall have been confined after your conviction and may the Almighty have mercy upon your soul.

Robert Nall was hanged on Saturday, 9 April 1842. He was thirty-three years of age.

## Alfred Waddington, 1852

Early in 1850, Alfred Waddington, a seventeen-year-old grinder, lived in Sheffield Park. He started courting voluptuously beautiful, sixteen-year-old Sarah Slater, who *The Times* described in December 1852 as being 'of considerable personal attractions'. Alfred and Sarah had known each other from childhood. Sarah worked at Butcher's edge tool factory in Eyre Lane, wiping tools and preparing them for sale. She soon became pregnant and before a baby girl was born in November that same year, Alfred had asked Sarah to marry him. Although she was fond of him, she was not impressed by his poor work record, or the bad company he kept; he had once stood trial for robbery. She told him she would only have him if he changed his ways, became steady and provided them with a home. Despite his sweetheart's obvious charms, this was not something Alfred found to be easily achievable without proper application and industry. By way of excuse for his own inadequacies, he convinced himself that the reason Sarah had turned him down was because she had a lover. Indeed, he informed her he had heard rumours that she had been in the company of a wealthy man who had taken her to The Great Exhibition in London's Hyde Park in 1851, an accusation that Sarah denied. It transpired at Waddington's trial that Sarah had indeed visited The Great Exhibition, but in the company of her uncle and aunt.

In December 1850, Sarah had brought affiliation proceedings against Waddington and he was ordered to pay two shillings a week for the child's support. Their relationship deteriorated and Waddington took to threatening Sarah with violence, even murder. In May 1852, it became necessary to take out a summons against him for assault and on 16 August she took out another for non-payment of the affiliation order. The little girl was at this time being cared for by Sarah's mother in Sylvester Street, while Sarah herself was in lodgings in Brown Street. Always trying to improve herself, she was working during the day and in the evenings attended reading classes at the Mechanics' Institute, with her friend Sarah Dobson. Early in the evening of 18 August, the two Sarahs were sitting on the doorstep of the house in Sylvester Street practising reading when ten-year-old Martha Barlow, who lived across the road, came to take the little girl out for a walk. The two young ladies left her to it and set off for their class at the Institute.

Martha Barlow took the child on a walk, the route of which passed some brick kilns. As she was passing them, Waddington appeared and told the little girl, 'I'm going to take the child for a ta ta.'

Martha told him, 'You can't, it's her bed time.'

Waddington snatched the child from Martha and ran off with her up Strawberry Hall Lane. Martha ran back to Sylvester Street to tell the child's grandmother what had happened, and the two of them went off in search of the toddler as darkness began to fall.

Sometime around 8.00 pm, Waddington called in at the Institute and sought Sarah out at her reading class. She went to see what he wanted and was met with taunts and threats concerning the whereabouts of the child. As the taunts continued Sarah followed him out into the street and Waddington tried to stab her in the side. She managed to escape from his clutches and ran off down Sylvester Street. A while later, Waddington came upon Sarah Dobson, who asked him, 'Where's Sarah Slater?'

Waddington replied, 'I've murdered her.'

He showed her his bloodstained hand, then pulled out a knife and slashed her across the face, causing a deep gash. Sarah ran off in fear of her life.

At 2.00 am, Waddington gave himself up to watchman Harry Soar and, holding out his wrists, told him to take him into custody. The watchman said he had no reason to do so. Then Waddington exclaimed, 'I've cut my child's head off!'

Watchman Soar took Waddington into custody and marched him off to the Town Hall. There was already a warrant out for his arrest for arrears of bastardy and Constable Jackson, who was on the desk, thought he was there concerning that matter, but Waddington soon put him straight.

'No, I've done something worse that will take me to York and hang me. I have cut my child's head off its body.'

He gave directions as to where the child's body could be found in Cutlers' Wood (near Heeley). He said he had used a shoemaker's knife to do the job and afterwards had thrown it into the river Sheaf near Turner's Wheel.

During a search that took place at around 4.00 am, the body of a female child was found. It appeared to be intact but when it was lifted up, the head fell off and rolled down the embankment. The child's body was found about a mile and a half from the Mechanics' Institute and a mile from Sylvester Street. The events that followed were extremely distressing. At the inquest held the following day, before Coroner Thomas Badger, Esquire, after the surgeon had given his finding following post-mortem examination, the child's body, stripped of its clothes, was carried into the courtroom in a basket. Waddington covered his face and turned away. Sarah was then brought into the courtroom and on seeing the child's body uttered several piercing shrieks and called out, 'My child! My child!'

She replied to a question from the coroner concerning the child's identity and, as she gazed at the pitiful sight in the basket, her beautiful features contorted in agony, said. 'Oh! Is he not a villain?'

Sarah was taken out of the courtroom in a state of collapse. The jury swiftly returned a verdict of wilful murder and the coroner was quick to write out a warrant for Waddington's committal to York.

Waddington took his trial in the Winter Gaol Delivery of 1853, before Mr Justice Talfourd. He was represented by Sheffield-born barrister William Overend. Overend's attempts to set up a defence on the grounds of insanity failed. At the conclusion of the evidence the jury retired at 1.10 pm and returned with their verdict of guilty of murder, at 1.55 pm. The judge, having donned the black cap, addressed Waddington, and while passing sentence his Lordship displayed great emotion and sobbed audibly:

Alfred Waddington, it is unnecessary for me to say a word with regard to the nature of the crime of which you are now to receive the last judgement of the law because I perceive that, almost as soon as the crime was committed, almost as soon as that guilty passion of revenge and jealousy which caused you to take the life of your innocent and unoffending child had subsided, which it did almost on the consummation of that crime, that you immediately awakened to a sense of the dreadful guilt which you had incurred and then sought to relieve yourself from unavailing anguish by making a confession of what you had done and giving yourself up into the hands of justice. I hope, therefore, that you are prepared to use for your everlasting advantage those few precious days which remain to you in this transitory life. I trust that you will so employ those days that you may obtain a portion in that pardon, which is held out to us through that great salvation which inestimable love has prepared for all those who seek it, which all of us need, and which may be extended even to you. As you will have during your few remaining days of your life the assistance of a minister of religion, who will with the greatest kindness endeavour to afford you consolations which your sad condition requires, and will wisely seek to promote your everlasting welfare. I can only now pray that the divine blessing may follow these endeavours. And to me nothing remains but to pass the sentence of the law, which is that you be taken hence to the place from whence you came and from thence to the place of execution and that you be hanged by the neck till you be dead and that your body be buried within the precincts of the prison and may God have mercy upon your soul.

When His Lordship referred to the pardon held out by Christ, Waddington himself burst into floods of tears.

Alfred Waddington was hanged on Saturday, 8 January 1853, before a crowd estimated to have numbered 8,000. He was twenty years old. His last words were:

Lord Jesus receive my soul.

Death was not instantaneous. He struggled for a few moments. Afterwards, his body was buried within the precincts of the prison behind the window of the condemned cell.

### James Barbour, 1852

On the evening of Thursday, 3 September 1852, two boys who were blackberry picking in Appleyard's field at Midhill Black Bank came across a man's body in a hedge bottom; the head and face were covered in blood. The body was placed on a cart and taken to the Royal Standard Hotel, where an inquest was later opened. A surgeon, Mr Roper, conducted a post-mortem examination and found a circular wound to the crown of the head, about 2 inches deep, and a similar wound behind the right ear. There were other superficial wounds and what appeared to be powder burns. When the skull was opened, gun wadding, fragments of bone and several flattened pieces of No. 4 shot were found in the brain adjacent to a wound at the back of the head; and some unflattened shot adjacent to the wound at the back of the ear. Other wounds and evidence showed that the wounds could not have been self-inflicted.

The dead man was subsequently identified as Alexander Robinson, a Scottish packman employed by a Doncaster linen draper named Barbour. Police enquiries established that Robinson had arrived in Sheffield on Monday, 30 August, taking lodgings at Naylor's, a public house in Watson's Walk. He stayed there until 2 September. During his stay, Robinson had met up with his employer's cousin, James Barbour, who up until August had also worked for his cousin as a packman but had been dismissed for embezzlement. There were many witnesses as to Alexander Robinson's movements and after extensive investigations had been conducted, James Barbour was arrested and charged with murder. He was tried in York at the Winter Gaol Delivery, before Mr Justice Talfourd, on Tuesday, 21 December. Having found him guilty, His Lordship addressed Barbour:

> You have been found guilty, to my satisfaction, of one of the foulest murders which the course of my experience embraces ... you for some secret grudge which you entertained against a man who was retained in the service of your cousin when you were dismissed – either for that or for a desire to possess yourself of some paltry gain, plundered his person and property. You sought an occasion to do this when he had completed his duties a Sheffield. You then led him away to a secluded spot and there either alone or with some confederate – alone as the evidence goes – you fell upon him suddenly and unawares, deprived him of life, sending him, without a moment's time for repentance of his sins or reflection, in the midst of youth – in the midst of life – in the midst of thoughtfulness to appear before the judgement seat of God. The law is more humane to you than you were to your unhappy victim ...

The judge having pronounced sentence of death, James Barbour was taken to the condemned cell. He was hanged on Saturday, 15 January 1853, and his body buried within the precincts of York prison.

### William Smedley, 1875

This case is notable for two reasons. The first is that William Smedley was the first person to be hanged at Armley Gaol since the coming into force of the 1868 Act requiring executions to be carried out inside prison walls; and also because he was the first of two Sheffield murderers bearing the same name to be executed at Armley. The second William Smedley, who was hanged in 1947, also turned out to be the last Sheffield murderer to be hanged.

The year 1874 started badly for William Smedley. His wife died and, not long afterwards, his eyesight began to fail. He was a table knife hafter, aged fifty-four. He had two daughters and two sons, but rather than go and live with any of them, he chose to continue to rent the house he and his wife had shared, in Apple Street, Harvest Lane. He engaged a recently widowed woman to clean for him. She was glad of the extra money as she had three children under twelve. Elizabeth Firth, as well as charring to earn a living, also worked at the local baths. Although she herself was regarded as being respectable, other members of her immediate family were not. Her late husband had served a prison sentence for larceny, her eldest daughter was a prostitute and one of her sons was known to the police.

As well as cleaning for Smedley, Elizabeth Firth was soon sleeping with him. He even went as far as to ask her to marry him but her youngest children proved the sticking point, which prevented the union taking place. As the year progressed, Smedley's eyesight deteriorated until he became totally blind. A course of treatment followed and his eyesight was partially restored. No longer able to continue pursuing his trade, he had to rely on a weekly handout of 3s 6d from the parish authorities. On Thursday, 26 August, Smedley moved in with his married daughter, Mrs Sedgewick; his furniture and belongings were moved out of Apple Street that same day. The following day he stayed indoors playing with one of his grandchildren until 6.30 pm, when he left the house and went to meet Elizabeth Firth. He turned up at her house in Bailey Fields and she invited him in.

At 8.00 pm the couple were drinking in the Bay Horse Inn in Pea Croft, drinking two pints of beer each. At 10.00 pm they moved on to the Harrow Inn in Harvest Lane, where they drank whisky and gin. When they left an hour later, both appeared to be sober. They walked up Apple Street together, where one of the residents, Sarah Ann Nutton, of No. 54, was looking out of her window and saw them standing beneath a street lamp. Moments later, she could hear Smedley's voice, and then Elizabeth Firth saying, 'No!' Followed by, 'No, never!'

There was then a noise, which was later described by Nutton as a 'great knock'. She saw Smedley take to his heels and Elizabeth Firth fall to the ground. Neighbours, thinking she was still alive, carried her into the Greaves Hotel. But in the light they noticed she was dead and had a great gash in her throat and a door key in her hand.

Smedley quickly gave himself up at the Central Police Station but not before buying a loaf of bread and some polony. When asked by his daughter the following day why he had done it and if it was jealousy, Smedley replied, 'Yes, I found something out and I loved her so much I did it. She was a good woman and I'm sorry I did it.'

It became apparent that Elizabeth Firth's death was as a result of a wound that ran from the left ear to the back of the neck and to the front of the throat. The trachea, carotid artery and jugular vein had all been severed. The woman would have been dead within two minutes.

Smedley was tried at Leeds on Friday, 2 December, before Mr Justice Lindley. The jury having found him guilty of murder, the judge donned the black cap and addressed the prisoner:

> William Smedley, you have been convicted by the jury for the wilful murder of Elizabeth Firth, and I for one am bound to say that I think no twelve reasonable men could come to any other conclusion than they did . . . there really is no evidence at all upon which any reasonable man could believe you were or are insane. Under these circumstances it is my painful duty to pass sentence upon you.

Sentence having been passed, Smedley was removed from the dock and taken by cab to the condemned cell at Armley Gaol.

William Smedley was hanged on Wednesday, 21 December by the old York executioner, Thomas Askern. As Smedley walked from the condemned cell through the yard to the scaffold, he passed an open grave, which within less than two hours he would occupy.

### Charles Peace, 1876
See Chapter 5.

### James Hall, 1881
See Chapter 6.

### Joseph Laycock, 1884
Thirty-eight-year-old hawker Joseph Laycock grew up in the Harvest Lane area of Sheffield. At the age of eleven he was working as an errand boy. Not long after, he turned his hand to

pot moulding before getting work at Kelham Island rolling mills. Never an industrious individual, he was not at all keen on any kind of work and turned to petty crime as an easier way of earning a living. He made his first appearance in court in 1871, and by 1884 had amassed thirteen convictions, mainly for drunkenness and petty theft. He also gained a reputation locally as a prizefighter, after he fought and beat a man from Leicester for a purse of a sovereign.

In 1875 he married Maria Green, and by July 1884, when the murders took place, she had borne him four children, and a fifth was on its way. Shortly before he had married Maria, Laycock had joined the militia, which meant he would disappear from time to time, and it gave him a convenient excuse for not doing anything approximating a normal occupation. At the commencement of what was to be a turbulent married life, Maria was quick to realize she could not rely on her husband for support because, if he wasn't incarcerated in prison, he was often away with the militia. The Laycocks lived at various places until settling in a three-roomed house at No. 2 Court, White Croft, near West Bar. To help make ends meet, Maria went out with her mother collecting bottles, which she would then wash and sell. However, despite her own industrious nature, she was not a naturally good mother; quite the contrary. She was far too fond of drink, preferring booze to childminding, and often left the children to fend for themselves.

Not only was Joseph Laycock a workshy shirker, he was also a drunkard and, possibly worst of all, a bully. Those who knew the couple could testify that Maria was an easy target for her husband when she was sober, being as quiet as a mouse; but when she had taken a drink she was a 'beggar to fight with'. Laycock tried to justify his ill-treatment of his wife by saying he was trying to break her of her drinking habit. The residents of White Croft had all too often witnessed his brutality towards her. He had twice tried to harm her, firstly by strangling her with his bare hands and, on a second occasion, with a garrotte. In June 1884, Laycock was sent to prison for twenty-one days for assaulting his wife. Within hours of his release, having returned home to White Croft, he had quarrelled with Maria and threatened to 'do for her'.

On the night of 10/11 July, Laycock murdered his pregnant wife, Maria, and their four children by slitting their throats. Next morning, the Laycock's neighbours noticed that their house was silent and shuttered, the keys were in the front door and there was talk of them have done a moonlight flit. Neighbours being what they are, by 10.00 am curiosity had got the better of them, and three of them, Mrs Kidnew, Mrs Carr and Mrs Blinn, entered the house. They immediately saw Maria Laycock lying in front of the fireplace in a pool of blood, her head having almost been severed from her body. Laycock was discovered upstairs with his four dead children, who had been similarly mutilated. Laycock had injured himself in the throat with the same bread knife he had used to kill his family. He survived to stand trial, which took place on Monday, 5 August, before Mr Justice Matthew. Several witnesses were called for the defence in an attempt to prove Laycock was insane at the time he committed the murders. The judge's summing up was more favourable to Laycock than might have been expected; but the jury were not swayed and returned after fifteen minutes with their guilty verdict. Joseph Laycock was hanged at Armley Gaol by James Billington (Laycock's being the first of Billington's 147 executions) at 8.00 am on Monday, 26 August 1884.

## Harry Hobson, 1887

Harry Hobson was born in Huddersfield but grew up in Sheffield's Button Lane. In 1887 Hobson was fifty-three and unemployed. He had originally worked as a grinder before serving in the army for fourteen years, being discharged in February 1868 with a good military character. In 1871 he married Margaret Wright in the Isle of Wight. She was a widow, her husband having also been a soldier, and at the time of her marriage to Hobson had a well-paid job as a cook at one of the principal hotels in Newport. The newlyweds moved to Sheffield, where Harry was fortunate to obtain a well-paid job as an engine tenter and caretaker, with accommodation and fuel provided, at Robert Thompson's horn works in Cambridge Street. The job was a cushy little number and enabled Harry to enjoy life and to drink. He had been a heavy drinker in the army and as time progressed his drinking increased.

*Cambridge Street, seen here in the early twentieth century. It was here that Harry Hobson lived and worked as an engine tenter and caretaker.* (David J. Richardson collection)

Thompson sold his horn business to his partner John George Stothard, who kept Hobson on. By this time Hobson was drinking to excess and had become insubordinate and quarrelsome. By September 1886, Mr Stothard had had enough of Hobson and sacked him. Hobson decided that Stothard's son, John Henry, was behind the sacking and told him, 'You will have to suffer for this my lad.'

Not only did Hobson lose his job but he and Margaret were obliged to find a new home for themselves. They moved into rented accommodation, a small dwelling at 3 Sands Paviours. During the next ten months, Hobson managed to find work for only one and the couple were finding it increasingly difficult to make ends meet. Margaret managed to get some work office cleaning and, according to neighbours, she kept her own little house spotless. Life with Harry Hobson could not have been easy for Margaret. He became increasingly morose and ill-tempered, and the neighbours were sure to keep their animals away from him lest he lash out at them with a kick.

Hobson remained resentful that he had been sacked and resolved to take his revenge. The Stothard's home was close by the General Cemetery, on the southern edge of the town, at 99 Montague Street. The household comprised four generations of the Stothard family: John George Stothard, the proprietor of the horn works, his wife, his mother, and his son, John Henry, along with his twenty-two-year-old wife, Ada, and their six-month-old baby. Ada had once worked as a domestic servant for the Stothards but since her marriage, those duties had been taken over by Florence Mosley, who lived in nearby Parliament Street.

At 9.10 am on Saturday, 23 July 1887, father and son, John George and John Henry Stothard, set off for the horn works in Cambridge Street. They left Ada and the young servant girl, Florence, working in the kitchen. At 10.30 am there was a knock at the door, which was answered by Ada, who was carrying the baby. Harry Hobson was standing on the doorstep. He asked if Mrs Stothard senior was in. Ada said she was and Harry asked Ada if she would tell her that he'd opened a rag and bone shop. He made small talk with her about the baby and then asked if he could have a glass of water. She gave him one and, after drinking it, he left. Ada then told Florence, 'That was Harry Hobson. He used to be engine tenter and caretaker at the works.'

Fifteen minutes later, while Florence was black-leading the fireplace, Hobson returned. He asked for a 'bit of cord'. Ada left the kitchen and went down to the cellar to look for some. Immediately Ada was out of the room, Hobson grabbed Florence by the head and aimed several blows at her throat with a knife, cutting her on the neck, shoulder and hand. Her terrified screams brought Ada up from the cellar. Hobson immediately turned on her, leaving Florence to make her escape. Florence rushed out of the back door and along the passage that led to the street, calling out, 'Pray come. A man is in the house and is murdering the missus and everyone.'

Help quickly arrived but Hobson had already done what he intended and left. Ada Stothard was still on her feet but within seconds she had collapsed on the floor with blood spurting from a wound in her throat. Her throat was bound in an attempt to staunch the flow of blood, but she was dead within minutes, Hobson having severed her jugular vein. Hobson was quickly apprehended and, following the usual procedures, his trial took place just fourteen days after the murder, on Friday, 5 August, before Mr Justice Matthew. Not surprisingly, the jury found him guilty. The following day, the *Sheffield Independent* newspaper included in its report:

> Justice has in this case been remarkably fleet of foot. Rarely, if ever has condemnation so followed a great crime. Fourteen days ago the family circle in Montague Street was unbroken and the hand of the homicide was still unstained with blood; now the wretched criminal is an inmate of the condemned convict's cell at Armley and little more than a fortnight will elapse before he pays the highest penalty that human tribunals can award to guilt.

Hobson remained indifferent to his fate. When the chaplain reminded him that his time of death was approaching, Hobson said, 'The sooner it comes the longer will be the rest.'

Harry Hobson was hanged by James Billington at 8.00 am on Monday, 22 August 1887, in the former treadmill shed.

### Robert West, 1889
See Chapter 7.

### Edward Hemmings, 1893
See Chapter 8.

# CHAPTER 4

# Murders in Sheffield during the Twentieth Century

## *Both sides of the throat had been cut, severing the jugular vein and exposing the bones of the spine . . .*

### Harry Walters, 1905

See Chapter 9.

### George Edward Law, 1913

Two and a half years before he committed murder, George Law had been taken in by the Cotterill family at their house at 17 Bamforth Street, when he was homeless and starving. Now aged thirty-four, he was back on his feet again, had a steady, well-paid job as a forgeman at the Weir Tilt and Forge in Warren Street, Attercliffe Road, and was well able to afford accommodation of his own.

On Monday, 20 October 1913, when he went down to get his breakfast he found a note waiting for him on the table. His landlord, George Cotterill, had already left for work. The note gave Law notice to quit the room that he rented. The Cotterills wanted the room for themselves, as George was having to share the room with Law, and his wife shared a room with their daughter. Given the circumstances, asking Law to quit was not an unreasonable request. However, Law didn't see it that way and was extremely disgruntled. He told Mrs Annie Cotterill and the Cotterill's daughter Edith that they'd have to carry him out of the house. He refused to go to work that day.

That evening, George Cotterill tried to talk some sense into Law, telling him, 'It's only right that I, the father, should have my own place. We have no accommodation for you.'

To which Law gave the reply, 'You'll have to carry me out, and don't bother hiding the razors. I have something better and sharper.'

Law then went out and returned, still uttering threats and rather the worse for drink. He continued to ramble on into the small hours. At 5.30 am both men got up. Law left the house at 6.00 am in his working clothes. George Cotterill left shortly afterwards and his daughter Edith, having taken her mother's breakfast up at 7.30 am, left for work herself.

When George Cotterill returned home at 7.00 pm he found the house in darkness and the back door locked. On entering the house and going upstairs, he found his wife Annie lying dead on the bloodstained bed in the front bedroom. She had a black scarf tied round her neck and severe head injuries. The police were called and the body was removed to the mortuary in Plum Lane.

In the back bedroom where Law slept were his work clothes; they were heavily bloodstained. In a pocket was found a note. It read:

Please Mr G.R. Cotterill, withdraw this notice or it will be the worse for you.
    From G.E. Law, the end of this.

A post-mortem examination was carried out at the mortuary in Plum Lane by the police surgeon, Dr Lane. There were several gashes to Annie's head, caused by a blunt instrument such as a file or possibly a heavy butcher's knife or cleaver. There were several cuts to the deceased's hands, which were in all probability defence wounds. Death was as a result of strangulation and loss of blood.

Law had gone to Mansfield to see his sister Polly. Having done so, he telephoned the police in Sheffield and told them of his whereabouts. He was tried at Leeds in the Winter Gaol Delivery, on Monday, 1 December, before Mr Justice Darling. Found guilty, he was sentenced to death. An appeal on the grounds of insanity was dismissed and Law was hanged at Wakefield Prison by Thomas Pierrepoint on Wednesday, 31 December 1913.

## Lee Doon, 1922
See Chapter 10.

## John William Eastwood, 1923
See Chapter 11.

## Wilfred and Lawrence Fowler, 1925

During the 1920s, trouble often flared up between various rival gangs prevalent in several areas of Sheffield and district but sometimes individuals were singled out, often for no apparent reason. Acts of violence were commonplace but in 1925, a more serious occurrence in Princess Street, Attercliffe, resulted in a man being stabbed to death within a few yards of his own doorstep. On the evening of Sunday, 26 April, there was an incident near the Windsor Hotel in Windsor Street that would lead to a fatal street attack the following night in nearby Princess Street involving members of the Garvin gang, known as the Park Brigade, which numbered Wilfred and Lawrence Fowler amongst its members. A stranger to the district was attacked and local resident William Francis (Jock) Plommer was summoned to his aid. This resulted in a fight in which Plommer got the better of one of the Fowler brothers, causing resentment among the gang members, particularly Sam Garvin himself, who was of the opinion that this was an opportunity for his gang to make their presence felt.

William Plommer lived at 42 Princess Street. He was thirty-three years old and worked as a labourer at Bessamer & Co. He had served in the army as a sergeant, was well built and had boxing experience. Plommer's rendering of assistance to a Garvin gang victim singled him out for special treatment. The gang members exposed themselves to closer scrutiny when, on Monday night, they were out and about in the public houses around Attercliffe and The Wicker asking for Plommer's address. Eventually they got what they wanted and by 8.00 pm there were at least ten gang members in the area and a crowd of onlookers. Plommer was a brave but clearly misguided man when he went out into the street. He offered to fight them one by one. But he was quickly knocked to the ground and attacked. He died shortly afterwards from two wounds to his abdomen between 5 and 6 inches deep. In addition, there were three scalp wounds, all about 1 inch deep. Seven Garvin gang members found themselves on trial for murder.

The trial took place at Leeds Town Hall, before Mr Justice Finlay. It started on 28 July and lasted for four days. The prosecution called fifty witnesses. Of the seven accused, two were acquitted, three were found guilty of manslaughter and

Wilfred and Lawrence Fowler were found guilty of murder. Their appeal failed.

On 2 September, it was announced that the brothers would be executed separately; Wilfred was executed the next day, along with Dalton murderer, Alfred Bostock, and Lawrence was executed on 4 September. Lawrence's pleas to allow him to be executed alongside his brother were ignored but the brothers were allowed to share the same cell on the night before Wilfred's execution. Their executioner was Thomas Pierrepoint.

## Lorraine Lax, 1925

Miner Lorraine Lax hailed from Woodhouse. He served in the First World War and in 1915 was badly injured during the Battle of Loos. He married Elizabeth Bedford of Darnall in April 1920, and went to live there at 71 Ripon Street. Within a fortnight he had left her and returned to his parents' home in Woodhouse. Elizabeth obtained a maintenance order against him but he was a persistent defaulter. After fifteen months, Lorraine and Elizabeth were back together again, staying initially with his parents, and then moving back to Darnall, this time to 54 Ripon Street. Neighbours witnessed many angry scenes between the couple. In 1923, they separated again and Elizabeth went to live with her parents. By this time she had borne her husband three children. Elizabeth then took a room in a house belonging to the Antcliffe family at 31 Ripon Street. Shortly before Christmas 1924, the Laxes once again became reconciled and Lorraine moved into the ground floor room with Elizabeth and their three children. Money was scarce and they were given notice to quit after they failed to pay the rent. On Sunday, 30 August, Elizabeth told her parents, 'I've got no money. We shall have to go to the workhouse.'

At about 6.00 am the next morning, Norman Antcliffe, the landlord's son, was upstairs when he heard a strange gurgling sound coming from the Laxes' room. Then the children began to scream. When Lax emerged from the room he was bleeding from a wound to his throat. The police were called and Elizabeth Lax was found lying dead, her body partly covered with bedclothes. Lorraine Lax was treated for his injury at the Royal Infirmary, where his wound was stitched. He was afterwards admitted as an in-patient to Firvale Hospital.

Police surgeon Dr Carter carried out a post-mortem on the body of Elizabeth Lax at Nursery Street Mortuary, finding that both sides of the throat had been cut, severing the jugular vein and exposing the bones of the spine, in which a broken piece of razor had become embedded.

Lorraine Lax was tried before Mr Justice Fraser at Leeds Winter Gaol Delivery on 1 December 1925. During the course of evidence, Lax gave his own account of the events:

> As I was getting up, I accidentally caught my wife on the shoulder and she said, 'You are up to your old games again.' I then crossed the room and when I turned round I saw my wife with a razor in her hand. I went across to take it off her and she struck out at me and wounded me across the right side of my throat. We struggled and I hit her and stumbled. I got hold of the razor and thrust it at her throat. I was not in full control of myself. I was very angry. I had no intention of killing her when I went across to take the razor from her. It was just done on the spur of the moment.

In his summing up Mr Justice Fraser explained the law concerning provocation, which might, in certain circumstances, reduce what would otherwise be murder to manslaughter. During their deliberations the jury came back into court and requested further clarification of the law of provocation. His Lordship told them:

> Great provocation reduces to manslaughter the act of killing, even though it may be done with some dangerous instrument such as is likely to kill.

The jury returned a verdict of guilty but with a strong recommendation to mercy. Sentence of death was then pronounced on the prisoner. An appeal was lodged on the grounds that the judge had misled the jury on the law regarding provocation and was heard on 21 December. It failed. Lorraine Lax was hanged at Armley Gaol by Thomas Pierrepoint, at 9.00 am on Thursday, 7 January 1926. He was twenty-eight years old.

## Samuel Case, 1927

George and Alice Mottram were married on 13 March 1926. George worked as a miner at Tinsley Park Colliery and Alice was a buffer girl at the Sheffield Plate and Printing Company works in Priestly Street. They initially lived in rooms on the manor estate before getting a house of their own in April 1927 in Ravencarr Road. The Mottrams were a quiet couple and away from work did not have many friends, saving Samuel Case, as when Case got married, George and Alice had been best man and bridesmaid, respectively. They would go out to the cinema and other places of entertainment as a foursome and visit each others' homes. Twenty-four-year-old, Samuel Case and his wife lived at 74 Woodhouse Road, Intake, and he worked as a miner at Orgreave Colliery.

On Thursday, 20 October 1927, George Mottram left the house at 12.30 pm, on his way to work on the afternoon shift. Alice was already at work. He finished his shift at 10.00 pm and caught the bus home from Darnall. He arrived at his house at 10.45 pm and was surprised to see that it was in darkness. When he tried the back door he was surprised to find it opened, as Alice habitually kept it locked. On entering the house and flicking on the light switch, he found Alice lying on the floor. Her head was near the kitchen table and her feet were pointing towards the scullery door. Thinking she had fainted, he ran for help, and saw neighbour Leonard Cutts, and said to him, 'I think my wife has had a fit.'

Cutts joined Mottram and both went back to the house. It soon became apparent that Alice was not ill, but dead. Her body was cold and around her throat was a towel. On closer examination they noticed a piece of knotted clothes line on top of the towel. Her spectacles were hanging from one ear and were broken. When a local doctor was called he pronounced life was extinct and thought she had been dead for about two hours. Dr Finklestone Saylis also observed that the dead woman's face was swollen, congested and of a purplish hue. There were no signs of a disturbance but Alice's purse was missing.

The empty purse was found on a piece of waste ground the following day by a member of the public. Police enquiries established that Alice had left work at 5.35 pm in good spirits with two workmates and was believed to have arrived home around 6.15 pm. A post-mortem examination established that she had been strangled.

The next day, Friday, 21 October, at 11.25 pm, Samuel Case walked up to Police Constable Kirbyshaw in Snig Hill and said, 'I want to give myself up for murdering a woman at Intake.' When cautioned by Inspector Flint, Case said, 'I murdered Mrs Mottram. I want to make a statement.' Case then proceeded to dictate and sign a written confession:

> I left home about 12.20 on the 20th to go to work but I did not go. I had seen Mrs Mottram on the previous day at her house about 6.45 and I then made arrangements to go again to her house on the following day. I went there arriving at 6.30. I saw a light in the house. I could see through a chink in the blind. Mrs Mottram came to the door and asked me in. I sat down but she did not sit down again for her tea but talked to me, the subject of the conversation that she was in a certain condition and I was responsible for it. She burst out crying. She knew I was responsible. She said how miserable she was and how she felt like doing what another woman did on the estate – drown herself in a bath. She said she was thinking, what would my wife and her husband think? We went on talking about the same thing. I asked her why she didn't finish her tea. She said she did not feel like eating, as all her thoughts were on what my wife and her husband would think. She said that she would rather be dead than her husband know. After she had said that, she bent down to put some coal on the fire. At that time I was standing with my back to the table and it seemed as if I lost control of myself then, for I pulled my scarf off my neck and put it over her head and round her neck, she was bent down at the time. Before I realized what I had done she was black in the face, on the handle of the door was a towel or tea cloth. I got hold of this and tied this towel or tea cloth round her throat. Then I saw a piece of rope on the floor and I tied that around her throat. After I had done that, I seemed to realize the seriousness of what I had done and my one thought was to get away. I noticed her purse on the table and it seemed to flash through my mind that if I took the purse, when she was found, robbery would perhaps be thought the motive. Then I switched the light off after I had picked up the purse. I have known Mrs Mottram about five

years. Her husband and herself, when my wife and myself got married, she was bridesmaid and her husband was best man. We have always been the best of friends though neither my wife nor her husband knew what was taking place between us.

Samuel Case was tried at Leeds Town Hall, before Mr Justice Roche, on 29 November 1927. The jury returned, after deliberating for thirty minutes, with a guilty verdict. Sentence of death was pronounced. An appeal was lodged, which proved controversial, as a known criminal from Liverpool named William Hartle made a bogus confession to the murder. Case was not reprieved. He was hanged by Thomas Pierrepoint at Armley Gaol on Saturday, 7 January 1928.

### Armin Kuehne and Emil Schmittendorf, 1945

This case involved foreign nationals who, while being held in a prisoner of war camp during the Second World War in Redmires, Sheffield, committed murder in March 1945. The murder occurred on 24 March, when a German prisoner, Gerhardt Rettig, was suspected by his fellow inmates of informing the guards of an escape tunnel being dug and was severely beaten, subsequently dying of his injuries at Wharncliffe Emergency Hospital at 8.15 pm that night. Four men were charged with his murder and taken to London, where they were tried before a military tribunal at the London District Prisoner of War Cage on 7 August. Two were found guilty of the murder, Armin Kuehne and Emil Schmittendorf, and were hanged on 10 October 1945, by Albert Pierrepoint at London's Pentonville Prison.

### William Smedley, 1947

The winter of 1947 was one of the harshest Britain had ever known and was certainly the worst winter in living memory. Thick snow was to be found in most areas for weeks on end, and there was a coal shortage. On the afternoon of Saturday, 8 March, at around 2.30 pm, like many people at the time who wished to keep their homes warm, eleven-year-old Peter Johnson was out looking for firewood among the bomb-damaged buildings in the city centre, along with his wood-gathering companion, ten-year-old Ronald Higgins. Peter was in one particular building in Spring Street, about 50 yards from the busy Bridge Street bus station, when on looking through a doorway he saw a woman's body lying face down at one end of the room. He called for Ronnie, and the two boys ran to the bus station to tell a bus man. Peter told the traffic controller, who sent for an ambulance and the police. Officers from the Central Police Office were in Spring Street within a few minutes and quickly realized they had a murder on their hands. The dead woman had been strangled with her own headscarf.

The dead woman was quickly identified, as one of the officers recognized her. She was a well-known local prostitute, twenty-seven-year-old Edith Simmonite, who had for the last six or seven years being living at a hostel in West Bar Green. She had not been seen since Friday evening. Several men who had been seen with the dead woman on Friday were identified, questioned and released. One man was thirty-eight-year-old miner and West Bar hostel resident William Smedley. He said he had seen her but had left her at 10.15 pm and had not seen her after that. He was interviewed again during the course of enquiries but stuck to the same story.

On Friday, 9 May, Smedley turned up at the police station and asked to speak to Detective Sergeant Naylor. He said he had some new information for him. He said after Simmonite had left him at 10.15 pm, she headed off in the direction of Bridge Street in the company of a man he knew by sight, but not by name, who was stopping in the same hostel as himself. This man had spoken to him, said he had murdered Edith and was clearing off to Rhyl. Smedley further said he had received a letter from the man asking him to meet him in Rhyl the following Monday. Smedley gave no explanation why he had not revealed any of this information earlier. The police paid him £3 for the information and told him he would be given £7 more if he kept his appointment with the man.

Smedley was taken over to Rhyl by police car for his meeting on Monday but the man never showed up. He and DS Naylor stayed in Rhyl until Tuesday, making enquiries to enable them to trace the man. On Tuesday afternoon they were in Colwyn Bay, when Smedley suddenly told the sergeant, 'I killed her.'

Smedley was then cautioned, and dictated and signed a statement:

> I went out of the Sun Inn with Edith Simmonite on 7 March at ten o'clock, and I was talking to her at the bottom of the hostel steps; she was nagging at me. I went down Spring Street at about 10.15. I went into an old building in Bridge Street. [Smedley then described a conversation that took place between him and Edith Simmonite.] ... I then got hold of her scarf and pulled it tight but I didn't mean killing her. She had the scarf round her neck and I pulled it tight in a single knot. I took the scarf round the top of her head but I cannot remember whether I tied the ends or not. Suddenly, she dropped back and stopped struggling. I got back to the hostel about 11.20. The reason I did it was she gave me a disease and was always tantalising me. My intention was to frighten her so she would keep away from me. I was getting fed up. I had a letter from an Irishman last Wednesday to go and see him at Rhyl outside the Yorkshire Miners' Convalescent Home. This man was at the hostel on 8 March 1947, and I told him I had killed Edith. I also told Matthew Frayne the same day. What I have written is the truth. I am not pleading guilty to murder but I admit that it was me who killed her.

William Smedley was tried at Leeds Assizes on 14 August 1947, before Mr Justice Pritchard. During his trial, Smedley admitted he had told lies to put police off the scent. Found guilty of murder and sentenced to death, his counsel advised him there were no grounds on which he could appeal. Smedley was hanged at Armley Gaol by Steve Wade on 14 August 1947. He was the last Sheffielder to be judicially hanged. His execution excited very little interest. Unusually, shortly after his execution had taken place, when the statutory notices were being posted at the prison gates, not a single person was present.

# CHAPTER 5

# Charles Peace and the Banner Cross Murder

## 1879

*Lacking one or more fingers of his left hand; cut marks on the back of both hands; cut marks on the forehead . . .*

Notwithstanding it being his birthplace, along with other strong Sheffield connections, including the murder committed at Banner Cross for which he was ultimately hanged, few names in the annals of crime are better known not only to Sheffielders but also to the wider public than that of Charles Peace. For decades following his execution, Peace's waxwork effigy and that of Police Constable Edward Robinson, who captured him in the early hours of Thursday, 10 October 1878 in London's Blackheath, were principal attractions in the Chamber of Horrors at Madame Tussauds' world famous waxworks exhibition. The exploits of this inherently villainous individual have featured in books, newspapers, comic strips and magazines throughout the world from late-Victorian times to the present day. Not merely for the despicable crime for which he was ultimately hanged, what has made the name Charles Peace so notorious were other curious incidents in his long career of criminality, perhaps the most shameful of which was when another man was sentenced to death for a murder of which Peace was guilty and at whose trial Peace was actually present in court as a spectator.

Charles Peace, more often than not referred to as Charlie Peace, was considered in late-Victorian England to be Britain's most notorious murderer, with the possible exception of the as yet unidentified and ultimately probably unidentifiable Jack the Ripper. Yet in the eyes of a large faction of the public who lionised him, Peace became something of a folk hero. So much so, the legacy he left in his wake resulted in this irrepressible felon and (at least) two-times murderer being remembered with affection and, by some warped individuals, admiration, rather than despised for the havoc he wreaked on the lives of respectable citizens and the foul deeds he perpetrated. Following his trial and execution, all over Victorian England parents used Peace's name as a means to bring naughty children to heel, uttering the threat, 'If you don't behave, I'll set Charlie Peace on you.' During the 1960s, a cartoon strip featuring Peace's exploits was featured in *Buster*, a popular children's comic of the day, more than ninety years after he was hanged. That he is, to this day, regarded by many as a celebrity, to me beggars belief. How on earth this grossly ugly (both in spirit and appearance), prematurely aged-looking, devilish little man achieved this degree of fame and became something of a romantic hero – and a lovable rogue – clearly deserves closer scrutiny.

*Charles Peace.* (*Illustrated Police News*)

Charles Peace was born in Angel Court, Sheffield, on 14 May 1832. His father, at one time a wild beast tamer with George Wombwell's menagerie, had settled down to work as a shoemaker and was well respected. He passed on to young Charles an interest in animals and a love of music. In early life Charles also developed a flair for the Japanese art of origami and became quite adept at creating artistic shapes from pieces of paper. He took a keen interest in amateur theatricals and learned to play the violin, becoming sufficiently accomplished to merit the accolade 'The Modern Paganini' on the playbills at local concerts. He was apprenticed at a Sheffield rolling mill, during which time he sustained a serious injury when a piece of red-hot steel struck him on his left leg and hand, maiming his hand and

*Hannah Peace. (Illustrated Police News)*

leaving him with two fingers short and a permanent limp. By the time he was twenty, Charles Peace had discovered that burglary was a far easier way of earning money than actually working for a living. Short in stature, as agile as a monkey and incredibly strong, Charlie wasn't very successful at first because between 1851 and 1866 he found himself behind bars on no fewer than four occasions, being sentenced variously to one month, four, six and seven years. Peace did not confine his activities to Sheffield but moved from town to town, often around the Manchester area. In 1859 he met a widow, Mrs Hannah Ward, who had a young son named Willie. Mrs Ward fell for Peace's charms and they married, Peace becoming stepfather to little Willie. They subsequently had a daughter, Jenny. They all returned to Sheffield in 1872, when Charlie's activities around Manchester were beginning to attract too much police attention.

During his exploits Peace had sustained a fractured jaw, which thereafter left him with the unusual ability of being able to alter the features of his face by protruding his lower jaw and suffusing his face with blood; changing to such an extent that he took on the appearance of a mulatto (the child of a black and a white parent). When he wished to adopt a more permanent colouration of his skin to assume a disguise, he darkened it with walnut juice. The pliability of his facial features enabled him to assume the most convincing disguises, foxing the police and the victims of his scams on numerous occasions. By this time he had perfected his technique in burglary and was generally admired by the few members of the criminal classes who were privy to his nefarious activities. The seeds of what was to become the legend that is Charlie Peace had been sown.

In 1875, Peace went into business. He moved with Hannah, Willie and Jenny to Darnall, then still a village, situated to the east of Sheffield, near Attercliffe. The Peaces took up residence at 40 Victoria Place, Britannia Road, where Charlie set up shop and traded as a picture framer and guilder. He also sold musical instruments and bric-a-brac. When committing burglaries, which he of course continued to do, he could not resist taking violins and other musical instruments. In fact, he became an avid collector. This passion for procuring musical instruments, more often than not by purloining them, was to remain with him for the remainder of his 'career'. Next door but one to the Peaces in Victoria Place lived Mr and Mrs Dyson and their five-year-old son. Arthur Dyson was a civil engineer who worked for the North Eastern Railway. In his early career he was in business in Sheffield and was the first surveyor appointed by the trustees under the Sheffield and Tinsley Turnpike Act. He later worked abroad. He was the son of Henry Dyson, a farmer and land valuer at Tinsley. Standing 6 feet 5 inches tall, with good manners and genteel disposition, Arthur Dyson had met and married his Irish wife Katherine when he was in America in 1866. Seven years later, they returned to England and before moving to Darnall they had lived with Dyson's mother in Tinsley.

It was not long before the Dysons became known to the Peaces, after Charlie was commissioned to frame four pictures, including one of Dyson's mother. Charlie was very taken with Kate Dyson from the start. She was a tall, buxom woman, almost twenty years younger than Charlie. She was rather too fond of strong drink and she and her husband were prone to having rows. By this time Charlie was forty-three, but looked considerably older. He had a tendency to stoop, and notwithstanding his limp, was also bow-legged. Despite what one might reasonably deem to be considerable shortcomings, it appears he was something of a charmer with the ladies and, when he tried his luck, Kate Dyson responded favourably. They took to going out together and were seen at various public houses, music halls and other places of entertainment. Charlie and Kate went to Sheffield Fair. They were even photographed together. The house that stood between their two homes was empty. It was in the garret there that they were able to indulge their caprices. Peace's fascination for Kate made him become something of a nuisance, at least to Arthur Dyson. He would call on the

Dysons whenever he chose to turn up, which was clearly not to Kate's liking as she took to sending her paramour notes informing him when Arthur would be out and not likely to return. By June 1876, Arthur Dyson had had enough of Charlie Peace. He made it quite clear that he was not welcome to call at the house any more. He wrote a note on a visiting card and threw it into Peace's yard. It read:

Charles Peace is requested not to interfere with my family.

On Saturday, 1 July, Charlie Peace came upon Arthur Dyson in the street and deliberately tripped him up. That evening, Charlie noticed Kate standing outside her house talking to three female neighbours. He walked up to them and demanded to know if they were talking about him. When Kate replied that they were, Charlie insisted on being told what had been said. When it emerged that she had been complaining about the assault on her husband, Peace pulled out a revolver and said in a menacing tone, 'I will blow your bloody brains out, and your husband's too!'

The following morning a magistrate's warrant was obtained for Peace's arrest, but the bird had flown. The Peace family moved temporarily to Hull, where Mrs Peace found work as a supervisor at some dining rooms. Charlie simply continued to fill the family's coffers by committing burglary at night-time, whenever opportunity presented itself, in Hull and wherever his fancy took him, and as usual he travelled extensively and even went back to Sheffield on several occasions, as his flair for adopting convincing disguises presented no barriers. He also spent some time around the Manchester area.

Arthur Dyson was relieved to discover that Peace had left the neighbourhood. He no doubt enjoyed the relatively brief respite he had had since his troublesome neighbour's disappearance. However, he evidently entertained some doubts about his wife's association with Peace and perhaps was not entirely convinced that this thorn in his side would not return. Clearly in an attempt to avoid this possibility, Arthur Dyson found his family a new home on the south-eastern edge of Sheffield in Banner Cross Terrace, off Eccleshall Road, about 6 miles from Darnall. Banner Cross Terrace stood on the left-hand side of the road in a secluded position, the gardens at the back being overlooked by the road from Sharrow to Eccleshall. Although the terrace was some hundreds of yards from the nearest other dwellings, it was nevertheless a relatively busy place, with regular traffic in the main thoroughfare opposite and a near constant flow of passers-by on foot. On 26 October, having sent their furniture on ahead in a wagon earlier in the day, they arrived at Banner Cross Terrace in the evening, when the furniture was still being unloaded. As the Dyson family approached the front door, Charlie Peace came out of the house to greet them. A heated exchange took place, which culminated in Peace telling Dyson, 'You see, I am here to annoy you wherever you go.'

When Dyson remonstrated with Peace and reminded him that there was still a warrant out for his arrest, Peace shrugged his shoulders and said he neither cared for the warrant nor, for that matter, the police. Clearly satisfied with the upset he had caused, Peace left the dumbstruck Dysons and called in at Gregory's, a grocery shop situated next door to the Dyson's new home, and bought some tobacco. The Dysons saw nothing more of Peace for more than a month.

While the Dysons enjoyed yet another Peace-free period, Charlie was going about his usual business and once again found himself in the Manchester area, where Irish labourers, the Habron brothers, John, William and Frank, were employed by a nurseryman and farmer, Mr Francis Deakin, at the well-to-do suburb of Whalley Range, near Manchester. They slept in an outhouse on their employer's premises. In July 1876, following a night of revelry, Police Constable Nicholas Cock had summoned two of the brothers for being drunk and disorderly; William received a fine on 27 July and the charge against John was dismissed on 1 August. Following the court hearing the brothers went to a beer house, the Royal Oak, where they were regular customers, to celebrate. After several pints, some comments were uttered against the police by the brothers, which in view of events that followed, later became construed as threats. That night, Constable Cock was on duty with Constable Beanland when they noticed a man loitering in what they considered to be a suspicious manner near the gate of a house in West Point, which until recently had been occupied by Mr Gratrix. The man was described later by a local man, Mr Simpson, as appearing elderly, with a stooping gait. The policemen separated to investigate and Cock followed the man as he entered the grounds of the house. Shortly afterwards, two shots were heard and when Constable Beanland and a passer-by, Mr Simpson, went to investigate, they found Constable Cock lying in the road, shot through the right breast. He died half an hour later.

Suspicion immediately fell upon the Habrons. Police were quick to call at the outhouses where they lived. They found them naked in bed and arrested all three of them. Their arrest was prompted by the police seeing a light as they arrived at the outhouses. This, they said, was immediately extinguished as the brothers heard footsteps approaching, clearly evidence of their guilt. The brothers were ordered to put on the clothing they had been wearing the previous day. They were arrested and taken to Northumberland Street Police Station.

When the scene of the murder was examined the following morning, a boot print was found in the mud. This was compared with a wet muddy boot worn by John Habron; it appeared to match. Some percussion caps were found in the waistcoat worn by William Habron. Frank Habron was later released but John and William were sent for trial at Manchester Assizes on 27 November, before Mr Justice Lindley. The prosecution maintained that one of the Habron brothers had shot Police Constable Cock out of spite and revenge. Various witnesses testified to hearing threats made against the police by the brothers and that William had inspected a revolver at an ironmonger's on the afternoon of the shooting. Despite the description given by Mr Simpson of the man seen at the scene of the shooting being elderly and stooping, Constable Beanland was adamant that the man had stood erect and definitely resembled William Habron. Francis Deakin told the court that he was convinced his employees were innocent. He had given the waistcoat to William himself and had probably left the percussion caps in the pockets. On 28 November, after two and a half hours of deliberation, the jury returned a verdict of 'not guilty' against John Habron. William Habron was found 'guilty of wilful murder, with a recommendation for mercy, on the grounds of his youth.'

William was nineteen years old. The judge donned the customary black cap and passed the mandatory sentence of death.

For three weeks, William languished in the Condemned Cell, until the Home Secretary, Mr Cross, saw fit to grant a reprieve on 19 December. The sentence was commuted to penal servitude for life and William Habron was sent to Portland Prison as Convict 1547. Throughout the Habrons' trial an elderly man with what could be accurately described as a stooping gait sat in the public gallery of the courtroom watching the proceedings with great interest. At the conclusion of the trial he left Manchester and went to Sheffield. The man's name was Charlie Peace.

The following evening, Wednesday, 29 November, Peace was in the vicinity of Banner Cross Terrace between 7.00 pm and 8.00 pm. He paid a visit to Gregory's shop and asked to speak to the proprietor (John Gregory), but was told he was out. Typically for Charlie in matters where the Dysons were concerned, he proceeded to make a nuisance of himself. Firstly, he asked a woman in the street if she would take a message to Kate Dyson for him, asking her to come and see him, but the woman refused. Not long before 8.00 pm he approached labourer Charles Brassington outside the *Banner Cross Hotel* and began to speak in disparaging terms about the Dysons. Brassington would have

*The Banner Cross Hotel and Banner Cross Terrace.* (The author)

nothing to do with Peace and moved away. At 8.00 pm, having put her son to bed, Kate Dyson came downstairs and went to the back parlour, where Arthur was sitting in an armchair reading. She sat down for a few moments and about ten minutes later, got up, put on her clogs, left the house by the back door into the moonlit night and went to the privy at the end of the terrace. A short time later, as she opened the door to leave the privy, she was confronted by Charlie Peace, who stood before her with a gun in his hand. Peace called out, 'Speak or I'll fire!'

Alarmed, Kate uttered a loud shriek, backed into the privy, slammed the door and locked it. Her husband, on hearing her anguished cry, left the house by the back door and, as he emerged round the corner of the building, saw his wife coming

*Peace confronts Kate Dyson as she leaves the privy at Banner Cross Terrace. (Illustrated Police News)*

out of the privy. He ran towards her, pushing past her as Peace fled down the passage. Dyson followed him, then crossed the forecourt and went down some steps, whereupon Peace turned and fired a shot at him. It missed but a second shot hit Dyson in the forehead and, as he fell backwards to the ground, his wife, who had followed them exclaimed, 'Murder! You villain! You have shot my husband!'

Peace fled, hopped over a garden wall and disappeared across a field in the direction of Greystones. In his haste to leave the scene he dropped a packet containing some notes and letters in a field belonging to Mr Else. These items included Dyson's visiting card to him. When examined by police it was observed that the notes were clearly written in a woman's hand and took the form of various requests or assignations. These, Peace later maintained, were Kate's notes and letters to him. Arthur Dyson was carried into the Gregorys' house before being transferred to his own house, where Dr Harrison, of Highfield, visited him and examined him as he was propped up in a chair. The bullet had entered his left temple and lodged in the brain. He died at 10.30 pm. Dr Benson arrived shortly afterwards and confirmed Dr Harrison's statement that death had taken place. Police Sergeant Bowler of the Eccleshall Division was in attendance throughout the night, along with constables Crowe and Sylvester. Inspector Bradbury visited the house during the night, and then went to make his report at the central police offices.

Mrs Dyson was sufficiently composed in the immediate aftermath following her husband's death to give an interview to a reporter from the *Sheffield and Rotherham Independent*. In what the reporter described as 'with a touch of the Irish brogue' she told him:

> Peace is a picture frame dealer by trade. He is a man of very bad character. He used to keep a shop in Scotland Street, or somewhere there, sometime ago. I dare say that would be a year and a half ago. About a year since that he moved to Darnall, and that is the first time we knew anything about him. He is about fifty years of age, about 5 feet 4 inches high, with a grey-white beard – full beard and moustache. When he came to live by us at Darnall he wanted to make

disturbances between me and my husband. He seemed at first to be a very kindly man, having birds and parrots and so on that he used to talk about. He enticed people to go in and talk. Mr Dyson used to go in, but after a while Peace seemed to put an evil eye upon us, and he then threatened my life. Mr Dyson is out of business. He has been a civil engineer at Tinsley. He is forty years of age. I have one boy, who is going on five years, and will be five on 11 December. Peace used to come listening at our door. Mr Dyson wrote him a note by postcard demanding him to keep off our premises, as he would have nothing to do with him. The neighbours told us he followed us about wherever we went. He once got up on the Nether Edge bus, and rode with us to Nether Edge, and he did it just to annoy us. One evening I was talking to a neighbour, and he came up. A friend of ours said to him, 'It is a shame, listening in that way,' and he [Peace] then came up and presented a revolver at me. That was on 4 July. I have witnesses to that. He presented the revolver, but he did not discharge it. It was a six-barrelled [sic] revolver. I then took out a summons against him, but he did not appear. A warrant was then issued, but he was never apprehended. He is a married man, with a wife and family, consisting of a son and daughter. His wife is bottle washer at Messrs White's liquor store in Church Street. His son is employed at Mr Ward's grocer's shop. His daughter is living at home, and I do not think she is employed any-where. Peace has been before the magistrates before, and they say he was in prison a year or two. We came to live here about six weeks ago. Peace was here the night we moved, and the neighbours tell us now he has been round our doors by day or at night, I don't know which. I went into the yard about a quarter-past-eight o'clock tonight. He was then lying in wait. He had been previously into Mr Gregory's, the grocer, next door. He asked for some tobacco and went out again. When I was coming out of the closet and was just opening the door, I heard a footstep and thought it was Mr Gregory's. Directly I had opened the door about a foot, I saw Peace standing there with a revolver in his hand. He said to me, 'Stand and speak, or if you don't I will fire,' or words to that effect. I screamed and shut the door. When I screamed Mr Dyson ran out. He had been reading by the fire, and he ran out in his slippers. I rushed out, and Peace fired, and it missed me when I banged the door. When Mr Dyson ran by he was shot in the front yard. He never spoke after he fell. I rushed to my husband to pick him up to see what was the matter. The neighbours brought him into the house and placed him on a chair. Dr Harrison attended. My husband's brother, Mr Henry Dyson, who lives at 17 Broomfield, also came to see him. Mr Henry Dyson is in the iron business at Messrs F. Hobson and Co's Saville Street. My husband fell on his back, with his head towards the road. The shot entered his left temple. Dr Harrison examined him, and saw that the shot had gone right through the brain. It did not come out, but got buried in the brain. Dr Harrison examined the wound, and told us to look after Mr Dyson, as he was in a very dangerous state. He was unconscious, and died a little before ten o'clock. Peace left Darnall when the warrant was issued, and we do not know where he went to live. I know of no reason but what I have stated why he committed the murder. He tried to make disturbances between me and Mr Dyson, and he did this because he could not succeed. The witnesses have heard him say he would blow my brains out, and my husband's too. He is connected with low, bad places in every city – Manchester, Liverpool, and the other towns. He told Mr Dyson so. Mr Dyson said he was a very bad man, which he knew from some pictures he saw. Peace wrote letters to Mr Dyson making out he was in Germany to put us off the path. That was when the warrant was taken out, and we knew nothing of him till we moved here six weeks ago. We removed here partly to get rid of him. He told Mr Gregory he should follow us wherever we went. He did not know Mr Gregory before. He has told people Mr Dyson owed him hundreds of pounds. He is a defamer and a murderer – that is the only name I can call him.

The inquest was opened on Friday, 1 December by the coroner, Dossey Wightman, Esquire, at the Banner Cross Hotel. On opening the inquiry the coroner said:

I need not explain to you why you are met here. This is a most lamentable case altogether. It appears that a man on whom suspicion rests, the man named Peace, whom in all probability you have all heard of, a man who is suspected at any rate of having caused the death of Mr Arthur Dyson, is not in custody, and the whole affair is so recent that I am exceedingly sorry to say I must adjourn the inquest. I know it is exceedingly grievous to the relations of the deceased, and if I could have seen my way to fulfil my duty and at the same time close the inquiry, I should have been very glad to have done so. But it is clear, it does not admit of a moment's doubt, that the matter is not thoroughly ripe for consideration. I do not know what may turn up, or what more may be known as to the particulars; but at any rate I am in hopes that the man on whom suspicion rests will be found before very long, and produced at the adjourned enquiry. He is entitled to be present if he turns up, and I should like to give him an opportunity of doing so. The question is, when will you have it adjourned to. I do not want a long adjournment. I asked Mr Bradbury to see what Mr Jackson [John Jackson, the Chief Constable] has to say.

Inspector Bradbury said, 'About a week or a fortnight; not more, and not much less.'

The coroner replied, 'That's my idea too. I think it ought to be adjourned for a week.'

Inspector Bradbury then handed the coroner documents concerning a letter that had been sent to the Home Secretary regarding the application to offer a reward for the apprehension of a murderer. The Home Secretary had ruled that the application could not be granted until the inquest had been closed. Having perused these documents, Mr Dossey Wightman spoke as follows:

I won't adjourn this for more than a week. I am willing to make it convenient for all parties if I can. Of course, Mr Jackson has a duty to perform with regard to this case, so far as the magistrates' court is concerned; and I asked Mr Bradbury to consult him as to how long he thought he should like an adjournment because, of course, if this man has to be apprehended, it is the duty of the police to find him and apprehend him. They seem to think a week will be sufficient. Therefore, I will make it a week, at the same time

and place. I suppose some of you come from this neighbourhood, and some from Sheffield? The bulk of them I
think from the neighbourhood.

Inspector Bradbury confirmed, 'From Brincliffe and Nether
Edge.'

The coroner then concluded, 'I will adjourn the inquest to
any house that is convenient to you. What do you say about the
Stag Hotel?'

This location being generally more convenient to the jury,
the coroner bound them over to appear at ten o'clock on the
morning of Friday, 8 December at the Stag Hotel, Sharrow
Head. The inquest was then adjourned. Immediately following
this, the jury went to Banner Cross Terrace to view the body of
Arthur Dyson, which had been laid out at his home there. His
widow then formally identified the body and the coroner issued
a certificate for burial.

On Monday, 4 December, the *Sheffield and Rotherham Independent* reported:

> The remains of Mr Arthur Dyson, civil engineer, who was
> murdered by the man Charles Peace, at Banner Cross
> Terrace, Eccleshall Road, on Wednesday night, were
> interred in Eccleshall Churchyard on Saturday afternoon.
> It was intended that the funeral should be as private as
> possible, and as the friends of the deceased anticipated that
> owing to the very great sensation awakened by the murder
> there would be a large attendance of the public, no precise
> announcement was made as to the hour fixed for the
> interment ...

The funeral was conducted under the auspices of Messrs Cole
Brothers of Fargate. The procession left the Dysons' house in
Banner Cross Terrace at three o'clock, the weather by that time
being raw and damp. Besides the hearse there was just one
carriage and that comprised an ordinary cab, there being only
four mourners, Mrs Katherine Dyson, her little son, and the
deceased's brothers, William and Henry Dyson. The plain
coffin, made by Mr Elliott of Banner Cross, was almost 7 feet in
length and adorned with a silver plate bearing the name, age and
date of death of the deceased man. Inspector Bradbury escorted

the cortège as far as All Saints Church, where Sergeant Bowler and Police Constable Holgate kept the crowd back at either side of the entrance. The crowd by then was much diminished from that which had gathered in the morning in anticipation of the funeral. After midday, when it was believed the funeral would take place, as the weather became even more gloomy than at first light only those with sufficient fortitude remained. The short procession arrived at the church, where the coffin was met by the vicar, the Reverend E. Newman, at the church gates. The bearers were made up of friends and neighbours of the Dysons: Mr Burnham, Mr R. Smithson, Mr J. Ogden, Mr G. Silcock, Mr J. Gregory and Mr J. Elliott. Several people were waiting inside the church and some others from the crowd of about a hundred followed the mourners inside the church to attend the service. As the coffin was borne out of the church and taken to the graveside, which was midway between the church and the road leading to the vicarage, the mourners were showered by a steady drizzle of rain. The widow wore a thick veil but even that was not sufficient to disguise her grief from onlookers. It was noticed that her face was bathed in tears as the ceremony drew to a close. Following the interment, Mrs Dyson and her son were escorted home by Mr William Dyson. Henry Dyson remained at the church to obtain the vicar's certificate of burial.

The inquest resumed on Friday, 8 December at the Stag Hotel. A full account leading up to the death of Arthur Dyson and the escape of Charles Peace was heard. Dr J.W. Harrison provided the medical evidence. He said:

> I was fetched about nine o'clock on the night of the murder to see Mr Dyson. I found him sitting in a chair. He was talking, but was insensible. As he was losing blood fast I had him immediately laid on a mattress, and then examined a wound on the left temple. He never recovered conscious-ness, and died in my presence at about a quarter to eleven o'clock. Mrs Dyson was present and also a man named Gregory. I have since made a post-mortem examination, assisted by Mr John Benson. I found a bruise on the nose and chin, as if the deceased had fallen on his face. The wound on the left temple was about an inch above the external orbit of the eye, and I could pass in the little finger

right through it to the skull and into the brain. There was a quantity of effused blood between the skull and the scalp. Upon taking the scalp away from the skull, I found a circular opening in the skull about an inch in diameter. The opening went through the anterior inferior angle of the parietal bone and also through a portion of the spheroid bone. The ball went through the brain in a direction upward and backwards through the left lobe, and was found lodged on the upper surface of that lobe. The bullet was flattened. The fact of it being so flattened is, in my opinion, caused by its coming in contact with the bones already mentioned. The bullet went obliquely and took an upward direction. From this latter fact, I imagine the man who fired the shot was in a lower angle than the deceased. The appearance of the bullet leads me to the conclusion that it was a conical one, but I cannot say it was so positively. I did not make a sufficiently minute examination to say whether the deceased was a healthy man, because the presence of the bullet in the brain fully accounted for death and for all the symptoms I saw . . .

In his summing up, the coroner said:

I do not intend to call any more evidence, as in all probability the jury will come to a conclusion with that which has been brought before them. As it is, there has been a very full enquiry into the death of the man Arthur Dyson. Inspector Bradbury, I am bound to say, has got up the case exceedingly well, and had anything about the matter and has brought forward apparently every person who knows anything about the matter whose evidence could be of the slightest importance in the inquiry. Indeed, the only thing he has not done, and that he ought to have, is to have apprehended Peace. I have no doubt, however, that he has tried his best to do so. The jury has first of all to consider how the deceased came to his death, and whether any party, and if so, who, was to blame in the matter. With regard to the cause of death, the jury will no doubt consider the evidence of the medical man, Mr Harrison, quite conclusive. Mr Harrison has made a post-mortem examination, and he has said the cause of death was a bullet to the brain ... You will therefore be satisfied the cause of death was the firing of a bullet from either a gun or a pistol, and that the question is, who fired it, and how came the deceased to be shot. The evidence is really conclusive, and I do not think I need to trouble you with any remarks about it ... You must consider whether you believe the man Charles Peace has been sufficiently identified before yourselves to justify you returning a verdict of wilful murder against him. Of course I need not tell you, as I'm sure you know sufficient of the law to understand that if the man Dyson was shot by Peace it was, and must be, wilful murder. Whether malice has been sufficiently proven before you or not does not matter. The law assumed that there was malice if a man killed another wilfully; and consequently the only verdict you should reach would be one of wilful murder. I think the only serious question you have to consider is whether the man was sufficiently identified to justify swearing that it was Peace who shot Mr Dyson ... All you the jury have to do is to satisfy yourselves first, as to whether Mr Dyson was killed by a shot, and if so whether you are satisfied that is the case then you can only return a verdict of wilful murder against him.

Mr S. Langstaff, foreman of the jury, stated that they did not wish to have the evidence read to them, inasmuch as it was very clear. Having retired for a few minutes behind closed doors the jury returned a verdict of wilful murder against Charles Peace. A reward of £100 was offered for his capture. Sometime after the inquest, Kate Dyson and her son went to America.

Sheffield Police issued the following description of Peace:

Very slightly built, height 5 feet 4 inches, hair grey; lacking one or more fingers of his left hand; cut marks on the back of both hands; cut marks on the forehead; walks with his legs wide apart; speaks somewhat peculiarly, as though his tongue was too large for his mouth, and is a great boaster.

Charlie Peace now used his considerable talent for disguise to its full extent to evade capture. In order to disguise the missing fingers on his left hand, he fashioned a tube that covered his entire arm, to which he added an iron hook. This gave the appearance that his hand and entire arm were missing. He darkened his skin using walnut oil and it was not long before he had established a convincing new identity. He acquired the nickname 'One-armed-Jemmy' and resumed his career as a burglar, travelling from Sheffield to Bristol, Oxford, Derby and Nottingham, before returning to his family in Hull, where his disguise even foxed his daughter, Jenny.

Peace continued to pursue his life of crime. In February 1877, while burgling the house of a man named Johnson, he was surprised in the act and, as he fled the scene, fired two shots at Mr Johnson, which fortunately missed the alarmed householder. Not long afterwards he was in Nottingham, where he became romantically attached to a young widow. Susan Grey was about thirty years old. She variously called herself by the surnames Bailey and Thompson. Peace was later to describe Susan as being 'a dreadful woman for drink and stuff'.

It was not long before she and Peace were living together as man and wife, calling themselves Mr and Mrs Thompson. He took Susan to Hull, where they took rooms in the house of a police sergeant. As usual, Peace resorted to burglary as a means of support. It was not long before the couple moved back to Nottingham, where one night police called at the house when Peace and his mistress were in bed. Somehow Peace persuaded the officers to leave the room while he got dressed and he promptly made his escape out of the window. He fled to London and found lodgings in Lambeth. Susan soon joined him. He took a shop there at 25 Stangate Street and traded in musical instruments during the day and by night he was augmenting his stock by breaking into houses and filching any instruments that took his eye, as well as money and other items of value. Within weeks of his arrival in Lambeth, Peace

*Susan Grey, alias Mrs Thompson.* (*Illustrated Police News*)

moved to Crane Court, in Greenwich, and afterwards, in the same district, he took a lease on two adjoining houses there in Billingsgate Street, where he installed himself and Susan in one, and, having persuaded his wife and stepson to move from Hull to join them, installed Hannah and Willie in the other (by this time Peace's daughter Jenny had married a collier named Bolsover). On 4 May, Peace was in Derby, where he robbed an outfitters in London Road belonging to Mr John Arthur Wailer. Concerning this robbery, Peace later commented, 'I done a very big mantle place in Derby for a great number of women's mantles and money . . .'

Later, in May, he took a lease on yet another property at 5 East Terrace, Evelina Road, Peckham. He called himself Thompson and claimed to be of independent means. Hannah, who used her previous married name, Ward, lived in the basement with Willie, ostensibly as housekeeper, and Charlie and Susan lived upstairs, where they lived in some style. The rooms were opulently furnished, mostly with items filched by Peace from other people's homes, or paid for with their stolen money. The house was a positive menagerie, being filled with an assortment of dogs, cats, rabbits and a variety of birds, including canaries, budgerigars, cockatoos and parrots. Mr Thompson would drive around the district in his pony and trap. He was well dressed and outwardly had all the signs of the respectable self-made man. He looked nothing like the Charles Peace who was wanted for murder in Sheffield. He had dyed his hair black, stained his skin and wore spectacles. Charlie also ventured further around south London to burgle by night. He ventured out of London to burgle, visiting such places as Southampton, Portsmouth and Southsea. As time went by the Thompsons became veritable pillars of the local community. They attended church on Sundays and held musical evenings, when Mr Thompson would entertain his guests by playing the fiddle, singing and reciting monologues. Peace spent time working on inventions and attached himself to a man named Brion, to whom he was known as John Wood. One invention, a device for raising sunken vessels, was actually patented. If on the surface all appeared well at 5 East Terrace, to the Thompsons' neighbours, the reality was that tensions ran high within the household. Susan was pregnant and she eventually

*Peace's London residence, 5 East Terrace, Evelina Road, Peckham.* (Author's collection)

gave birth to a son. She and Hannah had on more than one occasion argued, and following one particular angry exchange between them, Hannah divulged the details of the Banner Cross Murder. Charlie was highly alarmed at this and made both women swear on the bible not to reveal the secret to anyone else and to reconcile their differences.

Life in Peckham continued as usual until Thursday, 10 October 1878. Perhaps coincidentally or possibly because, as some believe, someone had tipped the police off, Peace himself maintaining that it was Susan Grey, there was an unusually large police presence patrolling the streets of the south-east London suburb of Blackheath. It was at around 2.00 am on 10 October that Police Constable Edward Robinson noticed flickering light coming from one room, then another, at the rear of 2 St John's Park, the residence of Mr Burness. Along with Constable William Girling and Sergeant Charles Brown, he went to investigate. While the sergeant went round to the front of the house and rang the doorbell, the two constables secreted themselves by the garden wall at the rear of the house. The moment the doorbell rang the dining room window was opened and a man climbed out. The man was none other than Charlie Peace. As he rushed down the garden path Police Constable Robinson went after him. When the constable was within 6 yards of Peace, Peace turned round and pointed a revolver at him and called out, 'Keep back, keep off, or by God I'll shoot you.'

Constable Robinson replied, 'You had better not.'

Peace fired three shots but all of them missed the constable. As Constable Robinson rushed at Peace another shot was fired, and this also missed its target. The constable seized Peace and there was a struggle, during which Peace called out, 'You bugger, I'll settle you this time!'

A fifth shot rang out and entered the constable's right arm above the elbow. Constable Robinson was determined to get the better of Peace and managed to catch him off balance, flinging him to the ground. He seized the revolver and hit Peace with it several times as Peace was reaching into a pocket for something and as he called out, 'You bugger! I'll give you something else!'

*Police Constable Edward Robinson struggling with Peace outside 2 St John's Park, Blackheath, at 2.00 am on Thursday, 10 October 1878.* (*Illustrated Police News*)

By this time, Constable Girling and Sergeant Brown had arrived at the scene and soon overpowered Peace. As he was being searched Peace attempted to escape but was thwarted by a blow from Constable Girling's truncheon. A few small items of booty were found in his possession, including a spirit flask and cheque book. He also had an array of burglar's tools on

his person, including a crowbar, jemmy and gimlet. While the
wounded policeman was taken to receive medical attention,
Peace was escorted from Greenwich to Park Row Police Station.
There he was charged with the wounding of Police Constable
Robinson with intent to murder. He refused to give his name.
Inspector John Bonney of Blackheath Road Police Station was
put in charge of the case. Later that morning, Peace appeared
before magistrates at Greenwich, where he still refused to give
his name. He was remanded for a week. A letter sent to his co-
inventor, Mr Brion, on 2 November, which Peace signed 'John
Ward' and in which he expressed concerns that he had not heard
from his family, provided the first clue to his identity. Mr Brion,
on learning of his associate's activities in Blackheath, set police
on the right track. It was, however, Susan Grey who provided
the true identity for him and it was she who subsequently
applied for, and was given, the £100 reward offered to any
person who supplied information leading to the conviction of
Peace. Peace's letters of forgiveness to her seem to indicate that
this was the case. On discovering that Peace had been arrested,
Susan and Hannah had removed as much as possible from the
house in Peckham. Susan, Hannah and Willie left London and
went first to Susan's sister's house in Nottingham. Hannah and
her son went on alone to Sheffield, where they decanted to
Mr and Mrs Bolsover's house in Hazel Road. The large boxes in
Hannah's possession, taken from the house in Peckham, were
found at Hazel Road on 6 November, after police investigations,
following a tip-off from Mrs Brion, had led them firstly to Susan
in Nottingham and shortly afterwards to Hannah. The boxes
contained stolen goods that linked John Ward with Charles
Peace. Although Hannah was subsequently tried on a charge of
receiving stolen goods, she was acquitted, as she was deemed to
have acted under the influence of her husband.

Peace was interviewed by Detective Inspector Henry Phillips,
the local head of the newly formed Criminal Investigation
Department of Scotland Yard. He was taken from Greenwich
to Newgate Gaol, where he remained until his trial. When
inspectors Bonney and Phillips went to make their report to the
Director of the CID, Mr Howard Vincent, the link with Peace
and the Banner Cross Murder at Sheffield was established.

Detective Inspector Phillips was dispatched to Sheffield to discuss matters with the chief constable there.

Charlie Peace was tried under the name of John Ward, alias Charles Peace, at the Central Criminal Court in the Old Bailey on 19 November 1878, before Mr Justice Hawkins, charged with the attempted murder of Police Constable Edward Robinson. Mr Pollard prosecuted and Mr Montague Williams defended. The evidence against him was so substantial it left the jury with no doubt that he was guilty, and having listened to the evidence, came to that conclusion after deliberating for only four minutes. Their verdict was delivered and the clerk of the court, Mr Reed, asked Peace if he had anything to say before judgement was pronounced. Peace then addressed the following remarks to the judge:

> My Lord, I have not been fairly dealt with, and I swear before God I never had the intention to kill the policeman. All I meant was to frighten him in order that I might get away. If I had the intention to kill him I could easily have done it. But I never had the intention to kill him. I declare I did not fire five shots. I only fired four shots ... If your Lordship will look at the pistol you will see that it goes off very easily, and the sixth barrel went off of its own accord after I was taken into custody at the station. At the time the fifth shot was fired the constable had hold of my arm and the pistol went off quite by accident. I really did not know the pistol was loaded, and I hope, my Lord, you will have mercy upon me. I feel I have disgraced myself and am not fit to live or die. I am not prepared to meet my God, but I feel that my career has been made to appear much worse than it really is. Oh my Lord, do have mercy upon me, and I assure you that you shall never repent it. Give me one more chance of repenting and preparing myself to meet my God. As you hope for mercy yourself at the hands of the great God, do have mercy upon me, a most wretched miserable man – a man that am not fit to die. I am not fit to live, but with the help of my God. I will try to become a good man.

Apparently unmoved by the remarks just made to him by the prisoner in the dock, Mr Justice Hawkins sentenced him to penal servitude for life. The judge recommended Constable

Robinson for promotion and for a reward of £25. Constable Robinson was duly promoted to sergeant. Following his trial Peace was taken to Pentonville Prison. Matters were already in hand to indict him for the Banner Cross Murder.

On Friday, 17 January 1879, Peace was taken from Pentonville Prison, where he was serving his sentence, and conveyed to Sheffield by train to appear at Sheffield Town Hall, before Mr Welby, the stipendiary magistrate, for a committal hearing. Mrs Katherine Dyson, who had returned from the United States of America to give evidence, was the first witness. It was decided that her cross-examination would take place at the next hearing and the proceedings were adjourned. Peace was taken back to London.

Early on the morning of Wednesday, 22 January, Peace was removed from Pentonville in handcuffs, and accompanied by two warders to catch the 5.15 am express to Sheffield for the second hearing. The train was due to arrive at 8.15 am. Peace had on his previous journey to Sheffield kept making excuses to leave the carriage to relieve himself whenever the train stopped. In anticipation of this occurring again the warders had provided themselves with small waterproof bags, which Peace could use when the need took him, and these could then be disposed of out of the carriage window. Shortly after the train had passed through Worksop, Peace asked for one of the bags. The 6-inch chain on the handcuffs Peace was wearing enabled him sufficient movement to attend to his own needs. He faced the window and duly emptied his bladder. As the window was being lowered in order to dispose of the bag, Peace leapt out of it. While one of the warders sprang towards him and caught him by the left foot, Peace grasped hold of the carriage's footboard and proceeded to kick at the warder with his right foot. There was insufficient space for the other warder to come to the aid of his colleague and the struggle continued as the train thundered on for another 2 miles, all the time the other warder desperately trying to pull the communication cord to stop the train, which for some reason would not activate. Peace eventually managed to kick off his left shoe, whereupon he fell to the ground as the train travelled on. With the assistance of passengers in other carriages the warders succeeded in pulling up the train. As the train continued on its journey the warders ran

*Peace escaping from the train.* (*Illustrated Police News*)

back along the line. Peace was found lying by the side of the track unconscious on the snow-covered ground. He was bleeding from a head wound. He regained consciousness shortly and was soon complaining that he was in great pain and dying from cold. He was taken back to Sheffield in the guard's van of a slow train heading in that direction, where they arrived at 9.20 am. News had already reached Sheffield Police Court that Peace

*The escape and recapture of Charlie Peace.* (*Illustrated Police News*)

had absconded from the train. The crowded courtroom heard the Chief Constable tell the bench that Peace had escaped. The court carried on with its normal business and sometime later heard that Peace was once again in custody but he had been injured and his attendance in court that day was unlikely. Peace received medical attention in one of the police cells from the police surgeon, Dr Stewart, and Mr Arthur Hallam, a surgeon from Sheffield. He had a severe scalp wound and was suffering from concussion of the brain. He was eventually pronounced sufficiently fit to appear before the magistrate on 30 January.

The public were showing considerable interest in the case and, to avoid the possibility of any scenes in the courtroom, the hearing was held in a dingy corridor outside Peace's cell in the Town Hall. Peace was seated in an armchair and grumbled often about the cold. He was represented by Sheffield solicitor William E. Clegg, whose claim to fame was having played football for both Sheffield Wednesday and England. In his cross-examination of Mrs Dyson, Mr Clegg set out to show that her relationship with Peace was of a far more intimate nature than she had been prepared to reveal and that Arthur Dyson had been killed in the course of a struggle in which he had been the aggressor. Mrs Dyson's inability to remember certain facts and her letters dropped by Peace in Mr Else's field as he fled from Banner Cross Terrace, some of which were read to the court, seemed to add credence to Mr Clegg's assertions. However, Mrs Dyson remained adamant in her denial that any struggle had taken place between Peace and her husband. The proceedings ended with Peace being committed to take his trial at Leeds Assizes. As Peace was escorted to the railway station to catch the train that would take him to Wakefield Prison, a large crowd had gathered to witness his departure. He appeared old and feeble and was wearing his convict suit, with its cap perched on top of the white bandage that bound his head and which contrasted sharply with his brown complexion. He remained in Wakefield until the eve of his trial, when he was taken to Armley Gaol in Leeds.

Charles Peace was tried at Leeds Assizes on Tuesday, 4 February, before Mr Justice Lopes (afterwards Lord Ludlow). The trial lasted one day. Mr Campbell Foster QC led for the prosecution and Peace was represented by Mr Frank Lockwood and Mr Stuart Wortley.

In his opening remarks Mr Campbell Foster contended that the shooting of Arthur Dyson by Charles Peace was premeditated and committed with 'malice of afterthought'. During Katherine Dyson's evidence, which was vociferously challenged by Peace's defence, Peace leant forward in his armchair, which was set within a semi-circular spiked enclosure, looking rather fixedly and occasionally summoning his solicitor and whispering to him. There were various witnesses who corroborated the events on the night of the shooting. Evidence was given concerning Peace's threats to the Dysons in July 1876. Then evidence concerning his arrest in Blackheath in October 1878, during which the revolver he had used was produced. There was tentative evidence that the rifling corresponded with the bullet extracted from the skull of Arthur Dyson and with the

*Charles Peace sitting in the dock at his trial at Leeds Town Hall. (Illustrated Police News)*

bullets fired on the night of Peace's arrest in Blackheath. In defence, Mr Lockwood addressed the jury in an attempt to persuade them that the death of Arthur Dyson was the accidental result of a struggle between Peace and himself.

In his summing up Mr Justice Lopes invited the jury to take the revolver in their hands, try the trigger and see for themselves whether they believed

*Kate Dyson as she appeared at Peace's trial.*
*(Illustrated Police News)*

the gun could go off accidentally. He said that Mr Lockwood had been perfectly justified in his attempts to discredit Mrs Dyson's evidence but that the case did not rest on her evidence alone. In his opinion it had been clearly proved that no struggle or scuffle had taken place before the murder. He urged the jury not to lay themselves open to the reproach that they had wrongfully taken away the life of a fellow man. He added that the plea of provocation failed altogether where preconceived ill will against the deceased was proved. He concluded by saying that if the defence rested on no solid foundation, then the jury must do their duty to the community at large and by the oath they had sworn.

The jury retired at 7.15 pm and ten minutes later returned with their verdict. They found the prisoner guilty. When the Clerk of Arraigns asked Peace if he had anything to say, he replied in a barely audible voice, 'It is no use my saying anything.'

Mr Justice Lopes then donned the black cap and passed the following sentence of death:

Charles Peace, after a most patient trial and after every argument has been urged by your learned counsel which ingenuity could suggest, you have been found guilty of the murder of Arthur Dyson by a jury of your country. It is not my duty, still my desire to aggravate your feelings at this moment by a recapitulation of any portion of the details of what, I fear, I can only call your criminal career. I implore you during the short time that may remain to you to live to prepare for eternity. I pass upon you the only sentence which the law permits in a case of this kind. That sentence is that you be taken from this place to the place whence you came and thence to a place of execution and that you be there hanged by the neck until you are dead ...

Peace remained composed as he was taken from court and back to Armley Gaol. It would appear that he took notice of Mr Justice Lopes' words to him regarding his preparation for eternity. He became thoroughly penitent. During his incarceration Peace was visited by the Reverend J.H. Littlewood, Vicar of Darnall, to whom he confessed all his crimes, including the revelation that four months earlier he had killed Arthur Dyson, and had shot Police Constable Cock at Whalley Range. He said that he had intended to break into the house but was spotted by two policemen. As he tried to make his escape he ran into Cock's arms. Peace said he fired his gun wide to frighten the constable but when he continued to come at him, he aimed straight and shot him in the chest. Peace said:

> I got away, which was all I wanted. Some time later, I saw in the papers that certain men had been taken into custody for the murder of this policeman. That interested me. I thought I should like to attend the trial, and I determined to be present. I left Hull for Manchester, not telling my family where I had gone. I attended the Manchester Assizes for two days, and heard the youngest of the brothers, as I was told they were, sentenced to death. The sentence was afterwards reduced to penal servitude for life. Now, Sir, some people will say I was a hardened wretch for allowing an innocent man to suffer for my crime. But what man would have done otherwise in my position? Could I have done otherwise, knowing, as I did, that I should certainly be hanged for the crime? But now that I am going to forfeit my own life, and feel that I have nothing to gain by further secrecy, I think it right, in the sight of God and man, to clear this young man, who is innocent of the crime.

Police needed to be convinced that Peace was telling the truth and not pulling a fast one by trying to get a convict free under false pretences. They interviewed him concerning the sequence of events on the night of the murder and drew a map of the area. He was able to describe his movements in such detail and pinpoint on the map exactly where and what had occurred that left no doubt he was telling the truth. A lengthy confession was written out by Peace concerning Habron's innocence. It ended:

> As proof of his inesence [*sic*] you will find that the ball that was taken from Cox's breast was one of Haley's No. 9 Pinfire cartridges, and was fired out of my revolver now at Leeds Town Hall ... What I have said is nothing but the truth and that is my dying words. I have done my duty and leave the rest to you.

Following Charles Peace's revelations, William Habron was set free and given a free pardon on 19 March 1879, and compensation of £800 'to ease his pain and anguish.'

Peace spent a great deal of time writing letters. He had forgiven Susan for betraying him and, although he desperately wanted to see her, had acceded to his family's wishes that he should not. On Monday, 24 February 1879, the day before his execution, Peace was visited in the condemned cell by Hannah, Willie, and his daughter and her husband. He was in good spirits. Before they departed, at his wife's request, Peace knelt and prayed with them all. As Hannah was leaving the cell, Peace handed her a card, which he asked should be printed as his funeral card. It read:

> In Memory of Charles Peace
> who was executed at Armley Prison,
> Tuesday, February 25th 1879.
> For that I don [*sic*] but never intended.

The following morning it was bitterly cold. Charles Peace rose at 6.00 am and spent some time writing letters. He ate a hearty breakfast, although he saw fit to complain about the quality of the bacon. Afterwards a warder rebuked him for the amount of time he was spending in the lavatory and banged on the door. On hearing this Peace called out, 'You are in a hell of a hurry. Are you going to be hanged or am I?'

When William Marwood, the executioner arrived, Peace remained calm. This is Marwood's own account of what followed:

> A firmer step never walked to the scaffold ... I admired his bravery; he met his fate like a man; he acknowledged his

guilt, and his faith in God with regard to his future was very good ... During the seven years I have officiated as executioner I never met a man who faced death with greater calmness. It's true he shivered a bit; but not through fear. It was a bitter winter's morning, and he complained of the cold ... The bravery was an outcome of his nature. He was ignorant alike of weakness and timidity ... He had been suffering with a bad cough for some days. The night before his execution he said to one of his warders, 'I wonder whether Mr Marwood can cure this bad cough of mine?' To which the warder replied, 'I have no doubt he could.' And I can tell you that a man who jokes about getting hanged to cure a cough is no coward ... he died instantly. But perhaps I had better tell you what occurred just before the execution: it is a most curious thing. He had got hold of the idea that I should terribly punish him at the scaffold and he repeatedly asked the chief warder to be sure to tell me that he wished for an interview about a quarter of an hour before he was led out to die. Accordingly, ten minutes to eight o'clock I went to the condemned cell, which stands about in the centre of the gaol, some 100 yards from the place where the scaffold was erected. Peace was seated, he was in his convict dress, and there were several officials attending upon him. The bandage had been removed from his head [Peace's head had been bandaged in consequence of the injury he received on the train journey taking him to be tried in Sheffield], and he did not wear spectacles. He was neither weak nor prostate, but sat upright in his chair, as if he had never known a moment's illness. When I appeared in the doorway, he seemed pleased, and holding out his hand said, 'I am glad to see you Mr Marwood. I wish to have a word with you. I do hope you will not punish me. I hope you will do your work quickly.' 'You will not suffer pain from my hand,' I replied; and then Peace, grasping my arm, said, 'God bless you. I hope to meet you all in Heaven. I am thankful to say my sins are all forgiven.' It was now time to pinion him. He stood up at my request, but did not really need the support of the two warders by his side. He was not at all nervous, and quietly submitted to my operations. Pinioning is a very ingenious process. I run a main strap round the body, and connected to it are two other straps, which take the small of the arm, so that the elbows are fastened close to the body and the hands are free. Peace complained, saying, 'The straps fit very tight.' I replied, 'It is better so; it will prevent you from suffering.' He made no further objection, and taking hold of the main strap, so as to keep my hand on him, we started from the scaffold. The Governor and the Under-Sheriff went first, then came the Chaplain; and I followed with the condemned man, two warders, attending him, one on each side. They grasped him by the arms, but did not support him. He was bareheaded. His face was pale, but pinched with cold rather than fear. As he arrived near the scaffold he gave a very wistful look at my arrangements. They were all right, and seemed to satisfy him, for he made no remark. He went up the steps leading to the drop with a firm tread, whilst the Chaplain read the burial service. I brought him to a proper stand under the crossbar, and then strapped his legs. When that was done he wished to say something to the reporters, and made a beautiful speech. Such a speech as never come from a condemned man I have executed. It was a really good speech. When he had finished it he asked for a drink; but you know that was unreasonable, and it could not be admitted, for the time fixed for the execution had fully expired. So I placed the cap over his face, and adjusted the rope, when he said, 'I say, the rope fits very tight!' I replied, 'Never mind; it's all for the best; hold up your chin,' and he did so immediately, so that I could properly fix the rope. 'Goodbye all; God bless you,' he kept saying as I went towards the lever. At this time he did not require anyone to support him, but I told one of the warders to take hold of the back strap. Whilst he stood in this manner on the drop with the noose round his neck, I pushed the lever forward; it withdrew the bolt from the swinging doors, and Peace's body fell through the aperture beneath the platform. The drop was exactly 9 feet 4 inches. Peace was dead in a moment; he never moved a finger or a muscle after he fell; so I carried out my promise to do it well and quickly.

*(Left) Peace writing his will in the condemned cell at Armley Gaol. (Right) The burial of Peace at Armley Gaol. A warder shovels quicklime into Peace's coffin.* (*Illustrated Police News*)

Following his execution, Charles Peace's body was allowed to hang for the customary one hour, it was then taken down and laid out. Afterwards, the body was viewed by the jury at the inquest held later that day. Charles Peace was then buried within the precincts of Armley Gaol.

# CHAPTER 6

# The Shelf Street Hatchet Murder

## 1881

*There are seven wounds, six on the head and one on the throat, going from right to left ...*

In 1881, a cutler named James Hall lived with his wife Mary Ann and one of their three as yet unmarried children, a daughter named Selina, in a short street situated off Leadmill Road, near the Midland Railway Station. It was at their home, described in contemporary accounts as a cottage, at 149 Shelf Street, that one of the most horrific murders to take place in Sheffield occurred on the night of Saturday, 26 March.

The Halls' home was situated at the corner of Shelf Street and Leadmill Road and was a very humble affair, comprising only a kitchen, living room and one bedroom. The entrance was in Shelf Street, and nailed on the back of the door was a horseshoe, for 'good luck'. 'Good fortune keeps the house the horse shoe's in,' so the proverb goes. The window that lit the small kitchen faced onto the back yard, the two other windows of the dwelling in the downstairs living room and the upstairs bedroom faced onto Leadmill Street.

James Hall, aged fifty-three, a spring-knife cutler, was employed at Messrs Thomas Turner and Co's Suffolk Works. At one time Hall was industrious, but more recently he had become somewhat workshy and some called him an idle dissolute fellow to whom loafing apparently came naturally. He could rarely be bothered to go out to work. Several of his neighbours didn't have a great deal to say in his favour. According to them his chief occupation was begging in the street and playing dominoes in public houses. He belonged to a fraternity of likeminded loafers who habitually stood at street corners with a halfpenny in their open hand begging for another to add to it with which to buy bread. By this method the 'beggar' usually had collected enough to keep him in beer for the night and the custom was always to keep a halfpenny with which to resume 'business' the following morning. His twenty-four-year-old daughter Selina was later to say that in the fortnight leading up to her mother's death her father hadn't worked at all and the most he had brought home during recent years was ten shillings last 'bull week'. The neighbours, however, if they had little to say in James Hall's favour, a man they generally regarded as behaving like a vagabond, they had nothing but good to say about his wife. She was a pleasant, hard-working woman who, despite her husband's shortcomings, made every effort to keep the family home together by taking in washing and doing other domestic duties around the town.

It seems that Hall was unable to appreciate his wife's self-sacrifice and industry. In fact, far from being appreciative, he became resentful, and as his drinking increased so did his moody fits. He had on more than one occasion threatened to murder not only his wife but also his daughter. This morbid desire seemed to seldom be far from his thoughts and a few weeks before the murder took place, Hall had once again threatened to murder his wife, and tauntingly had a hatchet sharpened for the purpose soon after his daughter had taken the edge off it chopping up fish.

On Saturday, 26 March, Hall passed the earlier part of the day drinking and returned home in a semi-intoxicated state at four o'clock. Mrs Hall was out working, charring for a Mr Sewell, in Broomhill, but Selina was at home. Her father was quick to ask what had been prepared for him for tea and expressed his preference for beefsteak, or at the very least, sausages. Selina told him he could have neither and as he had brought no money into the house he would have to make do with tea or dry bread and toast. He became angry and further demanded that he should be given beefsteak or sausages, then stormed out of the house and didn't return until well after eight o'clock. Selina was still at home and when Hall asked where her mother was, she told him she had gone to the shop to make some purchases and would soon be back. Mrs Hall returned and some angry words were exchanged. At nine o'clock, Selina left the house with her mother as Hall protested that his wife should not go out. Mrs Hall ignored her husband and went to visit her married daughter in Howard Street and then her son in Leadmill Road. Selina left the house to go out with her fiancé, Richard Duckenfield, a scissor grinder, who lived at 28 New George Street. She met him in the town and they went together to the White Hart Inn, in Waingate.

At eleven o'clock, a neighbour, Mr Benjamin Betts, was passing the Halls' house when he saw Mrs Hall leaning against the doorpost. As she rested her head upon her hand, she said to him, 'My husband has been striking me with a hatchet.'

Believing Mrs Hall to be exaggerating the situation as he saw no blood on her, and that the quarrel was not of a serious nature, Mr Betts replied, 'Oh, nonsense; go in and agree.'

Mrs Hall was not seen alive again, except by her murderer.

At 11.20 pm, Selina Hall returned to Shelf Street with her fiancé and found the door was locked. As Selina said goodnight to Dick, as she referred to him, she went to the back yard to get

*James Hall confronts his daughter, Selina, having murdered his wife, Mary Ann, with a hatchet.*
(*Illustrated Police News*)

THE SHOCKING WIFE MURDER IN SHEFFIELD

the key from a hook secreted near the kitchen window, where it was common practice to leave it when the family were out. On looking through the kitchen window she saw her father come from the front room into the kitchen. He was carrying a hatchet, which was dripping with blood. She immediately feared that he had done her mother some injury and let out a loud scream, which her father heard, and he rushed to open the door, possibly with the intention of making his escape. As Selina began to speak to her father, he aimed a blow at her with the hatchet, which with considerable presence of mind she managed to deflect with her umbrella, the blade striking her on the chin, and fortunately giving her only a slight cut. She screamed, 'Murder!' and her fiancé came back within seconds, having heard her first scream, and immediately sprang to her aid. He got her to safety and at considerable personal risk seized Hall as he attempted to strike him with a blow from the hatchet, wrestled with him, and succeeded in tripping him up and disarming him as he crashed to the ground, when the hatchet was forced from his hand. With the help of three other young men – Henry Mosley and Henry Merrill, of Matilda Street, and William Wentworth, of Fornham Street – who had heard the commotion and quickly arrived at the scene, they were able to prevent Hall escaping and kept him out in the street until the police arrived. Police Constable William Crowe was on duty in St Mary's Road. On hearing the cry 'Murder!' he hurried in the direction of Leadmill Road, where the cry appeared to have come from. On his way there he was met by a youth, who told him that a man had murdered his wife in Shelf Street. Upon turning into Leadmill Road, he saw Hall on the ground with Duckenfield and some other men holding him down.

The policeman entered the house and, on going into the living room, a gruesome sight confronted him. The fireplace was in the centre of the wall facing the door, with a recess at each side. In the recess between the fireplace and the window lay the body of Mary Ann Hall. She was lying almost at full length with her face uppermost and her head slightly twisted towards the wall. The head had practically been cleft in two, the whole of the right side caved in and brain tissue was protruding from her wounds. Her upper body was a mass of gore, and the paintwork, wallpaper and furniture were bespattered with blood. On satisfying

*The Halls' home in Shelf Street, which stood at the corner of Leadmill Street, with its door in Shelf Street and its living room and bedroom windows facing onto Leadmill Street. James Hall is seen pursuing his daughter, Selina, with a hatchet, with which he attempts to strike her. Selina fends the blows off with her umbrella, while her fiancé, Richard Duckenfield, comes to her assistance.* (Illustrated Police News)

himself that the woman was dead, Constable Crowe left the house and returned to Leadmill Road, where Hall was still in the clutches of Duckenfield and the other men.

Hall was taken to Highfield Police Station in London Road. He seemed unconcerned when he was arrested and during his removal to the police station he said very little. He was clearly under the influence of alcohol and during the journey said, 'I hope I have done the *****.' On arrival at the police station, he was asked his name in Inspector Bradbury's presence. He did not hesitate to give it, and added, 'I did it myself, and intended to do it.' The hatchet, which was smeared with blood, was also taken to the police station. When Hall was searched he was found to have a purse containing 10s 10½d in his possession. Inspector Bradbury then went to Shelf Street with Constable Crowe and some other officers. The police surgeon for the division, Mr William Dale James, was sent for and he arrived from his London Road residence and pronounced Mary Ann Hall dead.

James Hall was subsequently removed to the Central Police Offices to await his appearance before the stipendiary magistrate on Monday morning. On Monday, 29 March, James Hall appeared before Mr Edward Welby, at Sheffield Town Hall. The chief constable, Mr Jackson said:

> The prisoner is charged with the wilful murder of his wife. It will be necessary to have a post-mortem examination of her today. I shall be able to call one witness now, then ask your worship to be good enough to grant a demand. The inquest on the body of the woman has not yet been fixed.

Richard Duckenfield was then called. During the course of his evidence the chief constable asked him, 'When you heard her scream "Murder!" did you go back?'

Duckenfield replied, 'Yes; and then I saw the prisoner running after her with something in his hand, but I did not see what it was.'

Jackson continued, 'Did you see him do anything to the daughter?'

Duckenfield said, 'No; he ran after her but he could not catch her, and when I got nearly close to him he turned round and struck at me with a hatchet similar to the one produced. He did not hit me. I then ran away, and he followed me down the street. The daughter also came running after us, and she called out to me, "Dick, he has a hatchet in his hand." When she got nearly close to the prisoner, he turned round and was just going to hit her with his hatchet, when I got hold of his arm and threw him on his back ... When I got him on his back I struck him several times. The hatchet then had fallen out of his hand ...'

At the conclusion of Mr Duckenfield's evidence the chief constable asked for the prisoner to be remanded, and Hall was duly remanded for a week.

The inquest was held the following morning, Tuesday, 29 March, at the Royal Standard Hotel, St Mary's Road, before the coroner, Dossey Wightman, Esquire. The foreman of the jury was Mr William Monnsey. The prisoner was brought back to the hotel in a cab, accompanied by Detective Wormack. A large crowd had gathered outside the hotel in anticipation of his arrival. As Hall was taken out of the cab and into the hotel he was hooted and booed. Selina Hall was the first witness to be called. After saying that her mother was a healthy woman and that she had never had a doctor's bill in her life, she spoke about the events of the previous Saturday and, after saying that afternoon her mother was engaged in charring, added:

I was employed at Mr Ibottson's, edge tool maker, until half-past two in the afternoon. I left home at half-past eight in the morning. My mother was then in the house, getting her breakfast. I did not see my father that morning; he went out about half-past seven. When I returned home at half-past two, I found my mother ... I went out again into the next neighbour's house to polish a machine top, and I did not return to my parents' home until half-past four the same afternoon. I did not find anyone was in then, and I remained at home.

Miss Hall then described her father's return and him asking for beefsteak or sausages. She then went on to describe how he had left again in a temper. Under further questioning she was prompted to say, 'When he came in I went upstairs and he called to me. I suppose he thought mother was upstairs, because he shouted, "Polly, I'm not going out tonight." My mother was called Mary Ann, but he always called her Polly ...'

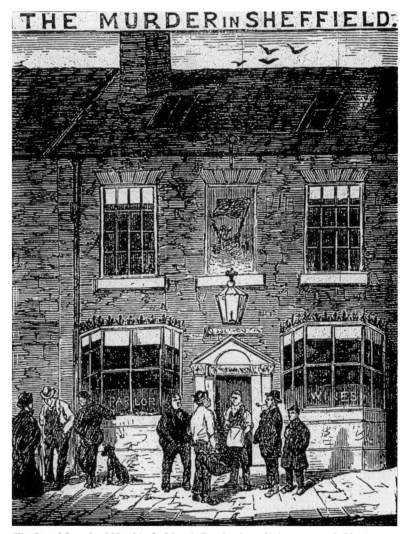

*The Royal Standard Hotel in St Mary's Road, where the inquest was held.* (*Illustrated Police News*)

Richard Duckenfield was the next witness called and he gave an account of his relationship with Selina Hall, which had spanned some seven years, as well as the events leading up to James Hall's arrest. The men who had helped him hold Hall until the police arrived were called next, and then Mr William Dale James, Police Surgeon. Mr Dale James said, 'I am a police surgeon and I never attended this woman during life. I did not know her. I have made a post-mortem examination, and I find there are seven wounds, six on the head and one on the throat, going from right to left. There is one on the right side of the head which has cut through the scalp 2 inches long, and cut a piece out of the skull.'

The coroner: 'Would that be a wound made by a blunt, dull instrument, or by a sharp one?'

Mr James: 'It must have been a sharp instrument. The wound next to that is 3 inches long, and passes through scalp and skull to the brain. It had also been done by a sharp instrument. The next wound is at the back of the crown of the head, and is one ¾ of an inch long, and passes through scalp and skull into the brain. The next forms nearly the whole left-hand side of the head. Nearly the whole of the left side of the head is destroyed.'

The coroner: 'Cut literally to pieces?'

Mr James: 'The whole of the left side of the head from the ear is cut away, probably the result of many blows.'

The coroner: 'Exposing the brain, or cutting part of it off?'

Mr James: 'Crushing it out, Sir, destroying it.'

The coroner: 'That is probably the result of many blows?'

Mr James: 'Yes. Then there is another wound below that cutting the ear in two, and cutting the top of the jaw bone and the bone at the back – the temporal. That is the left ear. There is another wound immediately below this, cutting through the skin and muscles of the neck, and has wounded the angle of the jaw.'

The coroner: 'Now in your opinion have all these wounds been done by a sharp instrument?'

Mr James: 'Yes. There is another triangular shallow wound on the left side of the neck. That hatchet [produced and shown to the jury] would produce the wounds. The body was otherwise healthy. The cause of death is the injuries to the head which I have described.'

The coroner: 'Death was almost instantaneous?'

Mr James: 'Yes.'

The coroner: 'You don't see anything at all improbable, supposing it is given in evidence that this woman had been seen a few minutes before the injuries, she might have received those injuries, and then been dead a few minutes after being alive and well?'

Mr James: 'Certainly.'

The prisoner: 'You say she had a stroke upon the head before eleven?'

The coroner: 'How can the surgeon tell you that? He cannot possibly tell it. He knows nothing about it at all except what he found at the post-mortem.'

The prisoner: 'He said instantaneous a bit since.'

The coroner: 'He said the wounds he saw were sufficient to cause death, but instantaneous is a very strong expression. [Addressing the witness Mr William Dale James:] Can you say within what time of receiving these wounds the woman would die?'

Mr James: 'By the time she had received all these wounds she would be dead.'

The coroner: 'In about what time would she receive them all?'

Mr James: 'There were seven blows at least, and with the destruction of the left side of the head, she would not survive that.'

The coroner: 'Then that is instantaneous?'

Mr James: 'It is.'

The coroner: 'You don't think it probable that she might walk out again after the first blows?'

Mr James: 'She might have after the first blow . . .'

The coroner: 'But you don't know where the first blow was?'

Mr James: 'If the first blow I have described was the first in point of time, she might have been able to walk out to the door, but she would not be able to walk after receiving all the blows. There would be no living after that.'

The coroner: 'You know nothing about the first or second blows. You know there are those marks on her head and that they have produced death. Mr Hall [the prisoner] wants to ask about a previous blow given in evidence by a previous witness. His witness [Mr Benjamin Betts] does not know anything about that, Hall.'

Mr James: 'There were some bruises upon the arms.'

The coroner: 'When you get a person with such injuries as these, I can never get rid of the idea that it is no good going in for these small bruises and contusions. Supposing there are contusions on the arms, it seems to me, if they were inflicted anytime before the 25th, they did not matter, because they would not kill the woman, and if inflicted on the 25th, they are so trivial as compared with the greater injuries which cause her death as to be unimportant.'

The prisoner: 'If I had never seen her about eleven o'clock, and somebody had done all this here ...'

The coroner: 'That is your lookout. If you can prove that, you will be a very lucky man but it will rest with you to prove it.'

Constable Crowe then gave his evidence, saying:

I went into the house and there I saw the woman lying on her back on the floor and she appeared to be dead. I then came out and got hold of Hall, and Wentworth assisted me in getting him up off the ground. I then took him into custody and conveyed him to the Highfield Police Station, straight off. I did not go into the house again then ... I returned to the house ... I saw the deceased ... in the same position in which she was when I was there before ... Inspector Bradbury was in the house and he sent me to fetch Dr James ... he pronounced her dead in my presence. That would be about half-past two o'clock on the Sunday morning ...

Inspector Bradbury: 'I came into the house. I saw blood and brains splashed upon the wall 5 or 6 feet high.'

The coroner: '5 or 6 feet?'

Inspector Bradbury: 'Yes, Sir, some of it was on the pictures and I should think they would be about 6 feet high up at least. I took her upstairs and laid her on the mattress, and sent for the doctor, I then returned to Highfield Police Station.'

Further evidence was given concerning Hall's condition at the police station regarding his state of intoxication. That concluded the police evidence. The coroner then addressed Hall, saying, 'You are entitled to give evidence or to make a statement if you like, but it is my duty to tell you that whatever you do say will be taken down in writing and may be used against you at your trial.'

The prisoner: 'Then I have nothing to say.'

The coroner: 'You are not bound to say anything unless you like.'

The prisoner: 'Then I'll save it to another day.'

In his summing up the coroner told the jury:

Your duty in this matter is to ascertain, as at every inquest, the cause of death of the deceased person; and secondly, whether any person or persons was or were to blame for the death ... it would be impossible for men in their senses to believe that a man could inflict such wounds on another person without intending them to lead to the death of that person. The evidence is so exceedingly clear that there really seems no point on which to direct you.

The jury left the room and returned after deliberating for ten minutes with a verdict of 'guilty of wilful murder'. The coroner then addressed the prisoner as follows:

The jury have returned a verdict of wilful murder against you, in this case, and it is my duty to commit you for trial for wilful murder. You will be taken from here to the Town Hall, and in all probability brought before the magistrate, after which you will have to go to Wakefield to await your trial at the next assizes for murder. It is a case in which you cannot have bail granted you, and, therefore it is not worth your while trying the matter at all, you will be kept in custody on this commitment until your trial.

*Edward M.E. Welby, Esquire (1836–1926), Sheffield Stipendiary Magistrate 1874–1914.* (Press Archive)

The proceedings lasted three hours. As Hall was brought out of the Royal Standard Hotel handcuffed to Detective Officer Wormack, a crowd of about 300 had gathered outside. As he was hurriedly taken to the cab, he was spat at by the women and jeered, booed and cursed for being a coward by the men. The coroner having made out a warrant committing him to trial, Hall was later taken to Wakefield Gaol.

Hall was brought back to Sheffield on 30 March, for another appearance before the stipendiary magistrate, Mr Edward Welby. At the end of the case for the prosecution Hall was formally charged with murder. When Mr Welby asked the prisoner if he had anything to say, Hall replied, 'It will not take me many minutes to say what I have to say ... it is stated by one witness that I have threatened my wife many a time in my life. That is true.'

Mr Welby: 'Do you wish this writing down?'

The prisoner:

Yes, it's true, I say. The reason was this. Three year sin' I lived on Paternoster Row. It wur a double house, front door and back kitchen door. There wur a yard behind and a passage coming into the street the back way to an entrance there. I went home one night, there wur no one in the house and the middle kitchen door wur closed. Well, I thewt where wur my wife. I tried to open t' door an' I couldn't exactly get it open, as there were summat behind. I pushed hard and as I go in't back kitchen door opened. My wife thrust me back into t'house through t' middle door. I thowt there were summat wrong so I went forward to t' back kitchen window and I see a man going down t' passage on his tip toes. Thinks I, 'That's William Lowe,' and I runs to t' bottom of t' passage and saw it wur him getting over t' wall into t' front street. So I goes back and says, 'Who were yon man in t' house wi' thee?' She says, 'What man?' I says, 'The man that's just gone out of t' kitchen door when I came in.' She says, 'There was no man with me.' I says, 'I see him going down the passage and leap over t' wall out of t' way.' She says, 'Who wur it?' I says, 'I know t' man.' I says, 'I know his first name but not his second exactly.' She says, 'It's queer it's queer you should know his first name and not his second.' I says, 'Why, because there's two half-brothers, both by one mother, but two fathers,' an' I says, 'I don't know which name is his, whether it's Lowe or Booth.' 'Well,' she says, 'there's been no one wi me.' I says, 'If I ever I catch thee at owt of sort I'll have thee life.' That's all about that. I've seen bits of things many a time after. I says, 'Don't let me catch thee else I shall do as I said.' Well I went home last Saturday night. Well, I saw her about a quarter past eleven and goes through t' kitchen into t' house. There wur a man and her on t' sofa. I says, 'What sort of game's this Poll?' I asked flying towards t' man to get hold of him. He kicks t' round table against me and flies out of t' door. I picks t' table up, runs to t' door but he has gone. I comes back and I says, 'Now what dost think about thyself?' She says, 'Now thou hast done as thou like, I shall do as I like.' I said, 'wilt thou?' 'Ay, lad,' she says. So wi me having a drop of beer I goes unto t' cupboard and gets t'hatchet and I says, 'I'll do as I like,' then I struck her. She fell on t' ground. I struck her again and again. Thinks I, 'Well she's dead.' Then my daughter came. The door was not locked. It sticks at times. I told her it was not locked. She called me a liar. I was agitated and I struck her.

Having finished speaking the transcribed statement he had just given was read over to him. Hall, on being satisfied that what had been taken down was absolutely correct, signed the statement with a cross.

The funeral of the murdered woman took place on Wednesday, 30 March, during the afternoon. A large crowd had gathered in Leadmill Road and Edmund Road in anticipation of the cortège passing by. Outside the cottage in Shelf Street where the murder took place and where the woman's coffin was resting, police found it difficult to keep the crowd from pushing forward, as it was estimated to number 3,000. As the coffin was brought out of the house and placed in the hearse, a sudden surge by those nearest the front strained police resources. They struggled to prevent some of the crowd pushing rudely against the relatives of the dead woman, as they were boarding the two omnibuses that had been provided for the mourners.

Into the first of the omnibuses the murdered woman's daughter, Miss Selina Hall, had to be almost carried, such was her grief. Miss Hall was supported by her suitor, Mr Richard Duckenfield, and her brother, Mr Abraham Hall. The mourners also included another daughter of the deceased, Mrs W. Travis, Mrs Abraham Hall (Eliza), James and Martha Gilmore, the deceased's sister and her husband, Mr James

Gilmore, Mr W. Hobson (brother of the deceased) and his wife, Mrs Mary Gilmore and Matilda Hobson, another sister of the murdered woman. Many other relatives also boarded the omnibuses. The cortège left Shelf Street a little before half-past three and slowly moved along Edmund Road, Shoreham Street, Queen's Road, then passed under the railway bridge at Heeley, before climbing the hill to the charge, where it arrived at four o'clock. The vicar, the Reverend H.D. Jones, was waiting at the gates. All along the route the streets were lined with onlookers. One woman was outraged that Hall had been placed in a cab after the inquest to convey him to the police station; she was heard to say he deserved not only flogging but roasting. By the time the cortège reached the church the crowd was said to number 5,000. Detective Wormack and several police officers kept the way clear. The large crowd of onlookers at the church gates remained orderly and showed a dignified interest as the coffin was lifted from the hearse and carried into the church. Only the mourners and press were allowed to attend the service, during which Selina Hall was much affected and her grief aroused considerable commiseration. As the coffin was carried to the graveside Miss Hall was almost prostrate with grief, and had to be supported by her brother and Mr Duckenfield. The grave, a family one, was situated on the hillside in the newer part of the churchyard. The crowd there was particularly loud but remained seemly in its conduct. As the vicar read the service for the burial of the dead while the coffin was lowered into the ground, the deceased's son, Abraham, wept bitterly. His sister Selina, now completely overcome, beat her breast hopelessly. When the gravedigger threw soil upon the coffin she called out, 'Oh, my mother, my mother,' and almost fainted. She struggled to the edge of the grave and gazed down at her mother's coffin for the last time. The plaque bore the inscription: 'Mary Ann Hall, Died 28th March 1881, aged 48 years'. On the lid was a wreath of daisies and some snowdrops. Selina Hall's friends thought it expedient to take her from the graveside as soon as possible. As they were escorting her back to the mourning omnibus, which was waiting at the churchyard gates, she fainted, and it was only with great difficulty that she was carried aboard.

After the mourners had left the churchyard, a large number of people went to the open grave to take a look at the coffin. Their curiosity having been satisfied, the crowd gradually dwindled away and only the gravedigger remained to carry out his duty.

On 29 April, Hall was removed from his prison cell in Wakefield and taken to Armley Gaol, Leeds. The following day he wrote this letter to his son:

> HM Prison, Leeds, 30th April, 1881
>
> Dear son,
>
> I now take the pleasure of writing to inform you that I am removed to Leeds hoping that this will find you quite well as it leaves me as well as can be expected. I inquired at the Town Hall if they had put your mother away and if they put her away in a decent and respectable manner and they said yes and I was glad to hear it and I thought that £8 pounds [*sic*] would be a nice sum to interre [*sic*] with and to put her away in a respectable manner and I hope her soul is in heaven God bless her and I want you to let me know who was at the Funeral and where they got their tea and who as [*sic*] took the house and I want you to write on sunday [*sic*] and then I shall receive it on Monday and let me know how you all 3 are so I beg to conclude with my kind love to you all and God bless you.
>
> From your affectionate father
> JAMES HALL
> For Abraham Hall
> 91 Leadmill Road
> Sheffield
>
> and I should like to see you on monday [*sic*] week

James Hall was tried at Leeds Assizes on Friday, 6 May, before Mr Justice Kay. Mr Charles Beilby Stuart-Wortley, MP, and Mr Ellis, appeared for the prosecution. Mr Vernon Blackburn and Mr R.W. Harper conducted the defence. The courtroom was packed and those who knew him well observed that Hall's stay in prison had told severely upon him. However, at the beginning of his trial he gave the appearance of being unconcerned. The prosecution's case was strong and they offered much the same evidence as was heard at the inquest. Several

other witnesses were called to give a more comprehensive background with regard to the murdered woman, the prisoner Hall
and their family, as well as those directly connected with the
events on the night of the murder. As his counsel, Mr Vernon
Blackburn, was addressing the jury, Hall gave way to tears. The
main thrust of the defence was that at the time his wife was
killed, Hall was in a frenzied state of jealousy. He had also been
drinking and either the drink or the jealousy, or a combination
of both, had produced a state of mind rendering him incapable
of knowing what he was doing, or indeed that what he was
doing was wrong, and he had remained in that same state of
mind when he spoke to the police. Hall wept throughout the
pleas being made on his behalf and continued to cry until his
Lordship had finished summing up, during which Mr Justice
Kay commented:

> I hope you will perform your duty with care, deliberation
> and courage. The statement made before the magistrates by
> the prisoner is one requiring careful consideration. In it the
> man made such excuses as he could for the deed, and the
> excuse he made was that of jealousy. He said he had caught
> a man in the house with his wife and it is for you to say if
> there is any foundation for him making the statement. Then
> was there any reason why he should strike the daughter? . . .
> You will have to consider whether the defence is sustainable
> or not based upon the evidence. It has been argued, and
> with thought, that the husband was in a frenzied condition
> of jealousy, that there was a hereditary taint in his blood,
> that his father had destroyed himself, and that he was not
> responsible for his actions. But it will not for a moment
> occur to your minds that jealousy, however well founded,
> could be an excuse for such a crime as this. The question is,
> not was he jealous or excited by drink, but whether these
> causes combined to produce such a condition of mind that
> he did not know the nature or quality of the act he was
> doing, or if he did know it, then he did not know he was
> doing wrong. At all events you must not be influenced by
> any morbid consideration for the prisoner. If you think the
> prisoner was in a frenzied state of mind, and that he did not
> know whether he was doing right or wrong, then you can

admit the defence; but if you are of the opinion that the evidence does not amount to that, you are bound to find him guilty. I am sure you will consider the case with care and deliberation, as I have tried to put it before you, and that you will consider it courageously, as Englishmen who have a very important duty to perform, both to the prisons and to society.

At 2.55 in the afternoon the jury retired to consider their verdict. They returned at 3.35 and found the prisoner guilty.

When the Clerk of Arraigns asked Hall why sentence of death should not be passed upon him, he replied, 'There has been some false witnesses that is all. If I had been allowed to speak I could have contradicted them.'

Having assumed the black cap, his Lordship proceeded to pronounce a sentence on the prisoner:

Prisoner at the bar, after a very careful inquiry and a very careful attempt to defend you, you have been found guilty of the heinous crime of murder. Your victim was your own wife. I have listened to the evidence with care, and listened in vain for any extenuation. I can give you no hope of mercy in this world. I implore you to use the time left to you, which is short, in trying to make your peace with God. There is mercy there for you, and for the vilest amongst us all. I can but tell you that that is all that is left for you in this world. I am bound to pass upon you the awful sentence of the law. That sentence is that you be taken hence to the place from whence you came, and from thence to the place of execution, and that you be hanged by the neck until you are dead, and that your body shall be buried within the precincts of the prison, and may the Lord have mercy upon your soul.

As Hall was removed from the dock he had once again assumed the appearance of being unconcerned, the same manner that was apparent at the beginning of his trial. Representations for a reprieve to the Home Secretary by Mr Vernon Blackburn were not successful and the date of execution was set for Monday, 23 May. Abraham Hall took a funeral card printed in memory of his mother to his father. On the eve of his execution, along with his final letter to his sister, Sarah, Hall enclosed the card and a request that the verse on his wife's funeral card should also be included on his. In the letter Hall withdrew the charges he had made against his wife:

Dear Sister,
I was glad to receive your letter and to hear that my children have reached home safely and that a lady had been so kind to ask them to have tea. I hope you will all be able to meet before eight o'clock tomorrow morning to pray for me the last time on earth. I wish to withdraw my words against my wife. I loved her dearly when I was sober and the sad reason it happened was drunken passion. I hope the Lord Jesus will forgive me for this and all my sins and that you will do the same. Please give my love to Mr and Mrs Allcock; good-bye to sisters, nephews and nieces, to Selina, Abraham and Martha and my last farewell to you all, from your affectionate brother.

JAMES HALL
Abraham, be steady, be steady

Hall requested that the following should be printed as his funeral card:

In Affectionate Remembrance of
JAMES HALL
who departed this life May 23rd 1881
Aged 53 years
Farewell, my friends and children dear,
You little thought my time so near,
Grieve not for me, grief is all in vain
Hope in Heaven to meet you all again

The following is part of a report by the journalist from the *Sheffield Daily Telegraph* who attended Hall's execution, which appeared in that newspaper on Tuesday, 24 May, the day after the execution:

At a quarter to eight o'clock, Marwood, who arrived at the Gaol on Saturday afternoon and did not leave the building until he had completed his task, entered the condemned cell followed by two powerful looking warders. On seeing the executioner with his pinioning straps in his hands, the prisoner raised his arms and uttered, 'Oh my God have mercy upon me!' He at once, however, submitted quietly to the pinioning process, which lasted only a few moments. At a few minutes to eight o'clock he was conducted from his cell, and the mournful procession left the corridor and entered the prison yard in the following order: First came Mr Keane, the governor of the gaol, then Mr Edwin Gray, the undersheriff, and close behind him Marwood and the prisoner, by the side of whom walked two warders ready to render him any assistance if their aid was required. Following these came sixteen other warders who fell in line by the side of the scaffold. On emerging from the door of the corridor the culprit came in sight of the scaffold, a high, black mass of wood and calico, erected in a corner of the prison yard, against the hospital, and some 30 or 40 yards from the wing in which he had been incarcerated. He started on seeing the erection but soon regained his composure, and walked with an unfaltering step. He paused at the foot of the steps leading to the scaffold, but only for a moment, for at a signal from Marwood, who was by his side, he mounted the stairs with a firm foot and placed himself under the rope, which had previously been fixed by Marwood and hung dangling from the beam above. As the solemn tone of the chaplain reciting the burial service fell upon the ear, Marwood, with a gentle hand, strapped together the culprit's legs at the ankles. The prisoner was at this time glancing around at the little crowd, composed of the officials and representatives of the Press, in front of him. Beyond a slight tremor on his face he appeared to be perfectly calm, and fully conscious of all that was passing around him. Marwood placed the white cap over the man's face, adjusted the rope, and moved the lever. In another moment there was a loud thud, caused by the falling of the drop, a lesser noise and the culprit had expiated the crime for which he had been condemned. The drop was about 9 feet. Mr Wright, who examined he body immediately after the fall, gave it as his opinion that death had been instantaneous, the man's neck having been dislocated by the sudden concussion. Nothing was to be seen but the swaying to and fro of the rope, the body being concealed from view by the black calico covering round the side of the gallows, which was the same erection on which Peace ended his life on the 26th of February, 1879. The body of Hall was allowed to hang the customary hour, and was then taken down . . .

An inquest was held before the Leeds Borough coroner, Mr Malcolm, at ten o'clock, at which, the governor of the prison, Mr C.A. Keane, was first to give evidence.

C.A. Keane: 'I am Governor of this prison . . . I saw sentence of death carried out. The body now viewed by the jury is that of James Hall, whom I received on 29 April.'

The surgeon, Mr C.J. Wright, then gave his evidence: 'I am a surgeon in Leeds and acting surgeon in this prison. I was present this morning when sentence of death was carried out on James Hall this morning by hanging. I satisfied myself when he was taken down he was dead. The cause of death was strangulation by hanging.'

The term 'strangulation by hanging' is an odd one to use, when one considers that Hall supposedly died an instantaneous death. That is according to what the surgeon, Mr Wright, reportedly told the assembled representatives of the press, as he emerged from beneath the black calico drapes that shielded Hall's weight was between 8 and 9 stones, according to the table of drops refined and perfected from Marwood's calculations. Marwood's methods were certainly more successful than most of his predecessors' but he was still refining his long drop technique, which he had introduced when he succeeded William Calcraft as hangman at Newgate in 1874. Marwood would point out to anyone who used the word 'hangman' when referring to himself, that Calcraft throttled the condemned, whereas he executed them. However, Marwood's methods weren't always successful. In May 1878, three years before Hall's execution, Marwood bungled the execution of Vincent Knowles Walker at York, when he gave him too short a drop and Walker died an excruciating death.

# CHAPTER 7

# Murdered in a Caravan
# 1889

*It's only the drink. I think the world of him and he would never hurt me ...*

Forty-five-year-old Robert West, who was born in Oxford, had been a travelling showman all his life. The *Sheffield Telegraph* described him as a very determined fellow with a firmly-set face that wore an expression of fierceness; he looked half-gypsy, half-horse dealer. Brought up on travelling from fair to fair, and feast to feast, in recent years his Aunt Sally stall, shooting gallery and swing boats had become a familiar sight throughout the Midlands and parts of Yorkshire. For several years he lived with a woman named Houlden, and she bore him three children. After her death he took up with the daughter of another shooting gallery owner, in Derby, and despite the girl's mother's dislike of her prospective son-in-law, Emma Sketchley, who was fourteen years younger than West, married him in 1877. In 1883, their first child was born and two more followed.

The Wests travelled with two vehicles, one being a two-compartment caravan for living in, comfortably fitted out with bunk beds and reminiscent of the type of cabin one might find on board an elegant steam ship of the day. The other vehicle was specially adapted to take the three fairground attractions. The Wests invariably travelled with two other showmen: Charles Warwick, Robert West's brother-in-law, who was married to Emma's sister, who ran a photographic van, and the Wests' longstanding friend, Thomas Twigdon.

The first rift of what was to become a regular feature between Robert and Emma West came late in 1888. It was at the Handsworth Feast that year that someone tipped West the wink that his wife was deceiving him, allegedly with a showman named John Baines, more commonly known as 'Leicester Jack'. West tackled his wife about this allegation but she denied there was any truth in it. Clearly he was not convinced that this was the case and relations soured between them. When he was drunk, which was all too often, the subject of his wife's infidelity inevitably came up and he regularly hit her. On occasions he had even threatened to kill her. In the summer of 1889, while they were in Derby, matters came to a head as West once more accused Emma of infidelity. He was arrested and the following morning appeared before the town's magistrates charged with assault and using obscene language. Emma came to her husband's defence, trying to get the charges dropped, but he was convicted and fined thirty shillings – or in default, six weeks' imprisonment. Emma paid the fine herself to prevent her husband's incarceration. Although she returned with him to their caravan, her mother persuaded Emma to leave West and go and live with her.

After a few weeks Emma went out on the road again with her brother-in-law, Charles Warwick, but fairs being what they were, it was almost inevitable that they would meet up with West again on the road, which they did, in August, at a fair at the Riddings, in Derbyshire. They agreed to reconciliation and West promised to behave better in future. So, the Wests settled down to travelling on the road again together, but it was not long, only a matter of days, in fact, before Robert West's jealousy surfaced again and the rows returned. By the second week in August, they were at Clay Cross and, during a row there, West once again threatened to kill his wife, which prompted Emma to tell her friends and travelling companions, 'It's only the drink. I think the world of him and he would never hurt me.'

The Wests moved from Clay Cross to Handsworth Woodhouse on Friday, 16 August, in readiness for the Woodhouse Feast, a gig Robert West had done for years, and he habitually pitched his caravan in a field adjoining the Royal Hotel. When the first van reached Dronfield, West told Emma to carry on to Woodhouse and pitch the caravan in Hawkesworth's field, while he went on to make some purchases in Sheffield.

When West arrived in a cab at the caravan at Woodhouse at about 9.30 pm, he was somewhat inebriated. After checking

*The market cross, Woodhouse. The Royal Hotel was where Robert West was drinking on the night he murdered his wife.* (Chris Sharp of Old Barnsley)

on the caravan he went to the Royal Hotel before moving on to the Cross Daggers. In the latter, where he stayed until closing time, West struck up a conversation with a showman named Benjamin Law. West was slumped on the table with his head in his hands. When Law asked him what the matter was, West replied, 'Oh Benny, you don't know. Benny I shall do the bitch tonight if they start on me.'

While West was out drinking, his wife was in her sister's caravan attending to her needs as she was unwell. Emma left her sister at closing time and went off to meet her husband, returning with him to their own caravan. As West went into the caravan his wife remained outside talking to Thomas Twigdon. After a few minutes, West came out and said, 'Emma, are you coming to bed?'

She replied that she would be in in a minute or two, and West said goodnight to both of them. Emma West joined her husband in the caravan after a few minutes and Thomas Twigdon returned to his own caravan, which was pitched nearby. At 5.30 am, Twigdon was awakened by a knock on his door. When Twigdon opened the door he was confronted by West, who asked him if he would get up, to which Twigdon replied that it was too early.

West's earnest reply was, 'Oh, but do get up I have something particular to tell you.'

When Twigdon asked what it was all about, West simply replied, 'Tom, I've killed my wife.'

Twigdon was disinclined to believe West, who reiterated, 'I've killed her. Come and look; she's dead in the wagon. She's in the wagon. Go and have a look.'

Twigdon would not do as West asked but asked him how he had done it, to which West replied that he had cut her throat. He admitted that he had done it soon after she had entered the caravan. Twigdon made the decision to go and fetch Charles Warwick. Before they entered the caravan, West said to Twigdon and Warwick, 'I want both of you to go with me to the police station first and I'll give myself up.'

However, when they arrived at the police station all the officers were out on their beats, so all three returned to Hawkesworth's field. Warwick suggested that they check to see that Emma West was really dead. When they looked in they could see the bed was covered with blood. Emma West was lying on the bed, dressed in her nightclothes, with her throat cut. Alarmingly, sleeping next to her was her young child, totally oblivious to its mother's condition and its nightclothes spattered with its mother's blood. Warwick gently picked the child up and removed it to his own caravan.

When Warwick returned he asked West why did he do it, to which question West replied that they had had a row and the result was that he had jumped out of bed and slit her throat. Soon afterwards Police Sergeant Ford, who was about his normal duties and totally unaware of the events at the Wests' caravan, came up to West, who was sitting on a wall, and West said to him, 'I have done it. You can take me and lock me up or do what you like with me.'

Sergeant Ford, believing that West was joking with him, told him to go home as he was not sober, to which West replied, 'Sober or not, I have killed her.'

At this juncture, Twigdon and Warwick appeared on the scene and confirmed the awful truth. Having briefly looked into the caravan, Sergeant Ford sent for help to the station and also for Dr Pillow. When the doctor arrived he confirmed that the woman was dead and had been so for some time. Soon afterwards, West was taken to the police station. On his way there, West said, 'This thing has been brewing twelve months. It will be next Sunday twelve months when we were here for the Feast last year when I began to find out her tricks. There's another I intended to do first, that Leicester Jack, and then her, but the bugger kept out of my way. I should have put his lights out first.'

On arrival at the police station he was charged with murder. When Police Superintendent Midgeley arrived he arranged for the caravan to be removed from the field into the yard of the George Inn. Emma West's body was taken inside the inn for a post-mortem examination in preparation for the inquest.

At 8.00 am on Sunday morning, West was taken by rail to Sheffield and transferred to the Central West Riding Police Office in Burngreave Road. On the journey there he said he did not wish to live any longer and he wished he could be finished off that day.

The inquest was held at the George Inn, Woodhouse, on Monday, 19 August, before Coroner Dossey Wightman, Esq., at 2.45 pm. The foreman of the jury was William Birks. Robert West, who had been brought there by cab, was seated in the corner of the room, well away from the windows. A large crowd had gathered in the street outside. The entire proceedings lasted under two hours, the coroner having declared that this was the simplest case of murder he had had to deal with during his long coronership.

*Dossey Wightman, Esquire (1836–1920), solicitor and partner in Wightmans and Parker, of Exchange Alley, Sheffield. Coroner 1873–1911.* (Press Archive)

Dr Henry Pillow, surgeon, said:

About 6.30 am on Saturday morning, I was summoned
by Sergeant Ford to see the body of the deceased at
Mr Hawkesworth's croft. It was lying on the bed in the van.
Deceased was dead, and in my opinion had been dead
about five hours. I examined the throat, and found a gaping
incised wound on the left side, extending from the ear
downwards, and forwards to the middle line of the neck,
below the larynx. The windpipe was not injured, but the
carotid artery and jugular vein were severed. That caused
death. It was a wound which might possibly have been
inflicted by the deceased herself. Judging from the evidence
I have heard, however, I should think that is improbable.

A long altercation took place between West and his mother-in-
law, in which West said that it was she who was the cause of it
all. At the end of the proceedings the jury returned a verdict
of wilful murder against West, and Mr Wightman signed the
committal warrant.

On Tuesday, 20 August, the *Sheffield Daily Telegraph* newspaper reported:

The sensation produced on Saturday at Handsworth
Woodhouse by the discovery of a horrible murder in a
showman's van had by no means subsided yesterday. On
Sunday thousands of persons visited the locality and
thronged the spot where West's caravan had stood. No
signs of the tragedy remained, but a morbid interest kept
people about the scene, discussing the murder from many
points of view.

Also on Tuesday there was a committal hearing before magistrates Sir Henry Watson and T.W. Cadman, Esquire. West sat
with his arm resting on the brass dock rail and his head in his
hands throughout the proceedings and maintained an air of
disinterest, although from time to time he moved in recognition
of old friends. Again there was a clash with his mother-in-law,
during which she said to him, 'You bad man, you murderer,
you villain. You ought to have your neck stretched.'

West replied, 'You caused three parts of it yourself. You have
no occasion to blame me. Blame yourself. I have done it and I

am very glad of it. I want to die, that is what I want. I am glad I have done it. I told you a long while ago I should do it and I have meant to do it.'

Mrs Sketchley then said to West, 'Villain! Blame yourself not me. And Leicester Jack. You and him, that is the two.'

The altercation continued and it became necessary for the bench to order Mrs Sketchley out of the witness box. At the end of the proceedings, having been committed to take his trial at the assizes, West called out to his friends in the courtroom, who included Charles Warwick and Thomas Twigdon, 'Goodbye all of you.'

On Wednesday, 21 August, the funeral of Emma West took place in Derby. The procession, consisting of the hearse and seven Broughams, left the White Horse Inn, Morledge, at 2.30 pm, the public house of the deceased's brother, Mr Samuel Sketchley. The coffin had been brought there on Monday night. The funeral was conducted by Thomas Lloyd of London Street, Derby, and officiating at the graveside at Nottingham Road Cemetery, Derby, was Primitive Methodist minister Mr William Marwood.

Robert West's trial took place at Leeds on 14 December 1889, before Mr Justice Manisty. Mr G.J. Banks and Mr W.W. Thompson appeared for the prosecution and Mr L.A. Kershaw and Mr Palmer appeared for West. There being not the slightest doubt that West had murdered his wife, the defence based its case on the prisoner's insanity. Thomas Twigdon in his evidence said that West suffered a bad attack of brain fever some seven or eight years before the event and had been told he should never drink. Twigdon said that up until 1888, West and his wife appeared to be very happy together but after he discovered about Leicester Jack, West began to brood.

The defence called only one witness, the prisoner's sister, Fanny Cooper. Mrs Cooper said that many family members had suffered from insanity. The prisoner's grandfather had been insane and had been incarcerated in an asylum in Abingdon until his death. His great uncle had to be strapped down to his bed because of insanity and a cousin also suffered from insanity. Mrs Cooper admitted that she had not seen her brother for twenty years but said that when she had known him he displayed the same signs of insanity as other members of her family.

Mr Kershaw, addressing the jury, said:

> There is not the slightest doubt that the prisoner murdered his wife but I must ask you to say it was done in a moment of insanity, his blood having been raised to a pitch of excitement by long brooding over the ills which had been wrought to his domestic peace by Leicester Jack. It was at Handsworth where his peace of mind was first destroyed and on returning to the place after an absence of twelve months, it is not difficult to understand that the germ of insanity within him was roused by the terrible thought of the wrong that had been done to him and sprang into full being in one round. Reason for the time being was thrown from her seat and the prisoner for the time being was in the grasp of an insane impulse – an impulse which he followed blindly to whatever end it might tend. In the present case the man's hand turned against the one whom he loved best in the world, and I would remind you that, prior to the time when he began to doubt the fidelity of his wife, he loved her, as you were told by Twigdon, more than life.

For the prosecution Banks submitted that the evidence brought by the defence did not show that the prisoner was insane, and supposing every word spoken by Mrs Cooper was true, there was no evidence to show that West had been otherwise than perfectly sane for the last twenty years. In his summing up, Mr Justice Manisty directed the jury that drunkenness was no excuse for the prisoner having committed a crime, and also there was no evidence of apparent insanity in the prisoner, though no doubt there was evidence of insanity in the family.

The jury retired to consider the evidence and returned shortly with a verdict of guilty, with a strong recommendation to mercy on account of the great provocation he had received. As was customary, His Lordship donned the black cap, and then told West:

> Robert West, you have been found guilty of the murder of your wife. It is not for me to make any observations on the

heinousness of that crime. The law imposes on me one duty and one only and that is to pass sentence of death.

Robert West did not receive a reprieve. He resigned himself to his fate and while he awaited his execution he was attended by the prison chaplain at Armley, Reverend Dr Bowlam. He was hanged by James Billington on 31 December 1889, together with a thirty-nine-year-old Halifax murderer, Frederick Brett.

# CHAPTER 8

# The Woodhouse Murder
# 1893

## *Mrs Fox ... told him she thought he would have drowned himself, to which Hemmings replied he thought too much about himself to do that ...*

On Thursday, 16 February 1893, Mrs Annie Hemmings should have been celebrating her twenty-first birthday. Instead of being a day filled with joy for her, an entirely different fate was in store, for she was to suffer a violent end at the hands of her husband.

Born Annie Hague, she hailed from Normanton, near Wakefield, and had been married at All Saints' Church there, on 4 June the previous year. The marriage certificate described her husband, Edward Hemmings, of 43 Benson Lane, as a collier, and herself, Annie Hague, as a spinster. Various accounts indicated that the couple were mismatched from the start. Annie had earned a reputation for hard work and honesty when, after leaving school, she took her first job as a general servant at The Huntsman public house. Good looking and gregarious by nature, she was regarded by some as a bit of a flirt. She was cheerful, light-hearted, chatty and high-spirited. She did, however, have a quick temper. She was also fond of pretty clothes. Despite having been brought up in a deeply religious household, Ted Hemmings was not without his faults. By temperament he was morose, sullen and melancholy. Those who knew him well described Hemmings as being moody and self-contained. He sometimes had to be asked a question five or six times before he would answer and he was apt to brood over fancied grievances and nurse the spirit of revenge. Hemmings' feelings for his wife tended to manifest extreme jealousy within himself whenever she became too friendly towards another man, even if that man should be a relative.

Up to the time he committed murder he had a clean record. His principal failing was that he was not an industrious man. Unbeknown to his soon-to-be wife, he shirked work whenever possible, resulting in him being short of money and, not long after their marriage, Annie was shocked to discover that her new husband was heavily in debt. Indeed, in the months that followed, much of the furniture they acquired on hire purchase was repossessed due to Hemmings' inability to meet the instalment payments. Hemmings was so averse to having to work for a living that he relied on others to knock him up, otherwise he simply didn't go.

Most likely in an attempt to escape creditors, Edward and Annie Hemmings moved from Normanton to Woodhouse on 20 August and lodged for a few weeks with Annie's sister, Anice Jones, at Canary Island, Woodhouse Mill. Once Hemmings had found work at Birley Colliery, they took lodgings in Robin Lane, Beighton, buying furniture on hire purchase. Within two weeks the couple had quarrelled and Ted had walked out, leaving Annie to support herself by whatever means she could. Reduced to scraping a living by taking in her neighbours' washing, Annie was unable to pay the instalments and her new furniture was taken back to the department store from which it had only recently been purchased.

During this temporary absence from his wife, Hemmings revealed to his sister-in-law, as he was subsequently to reveal to others, the depth of his jealousy. Indeed, he confided to Anice Jones that he worshipped the ground his wife walked on. Ominously, he added that he could not bear to see Annie talking to another man. He said he would sooner kill her than see her do so and would think nothing of it. He produced a razor from his pocket with which he said he would cut Annie's throat and then his own. Annie told her sister that the quarrels stemmed from the fact that Ted was idle and would do nothing without being pushed along. By February 1893, Annie and Ted Hemmings had become reconciled and had moved into lodgings in Furnace Lane, Woodhouse, a house they shared with its owners, Mr and Mrs Kennington, and three other lodgers. Mr Kennington was a shunter at Beighton Railway Station.

This was to be the Hemmings' last marital home. Ted Hemmings, who was now working at Treeton Colliery, continued to visit his sister-in-law and to pour out his tale of woes. He told Mrs Jones that when they first moved into the Kennington's house their marital problems appeared to be at an end, but as time progressed, Annie seemed to prefer spending time with the other lodgers than keeping him company. He said that she treated him like a dog.

At about 2.45 am on the morning of Thursday, 16 February 1893, one of the lodgers at the house in Furnace Lane, George Bradshaw, heard a woman's scream. He went to the landing and called out to see if all was well. Ted Hemmings replied to assure him that it was, so Mr Bradshaw went back to bed. At about four o'clock he heard someone leaving the house. He believed it was Ted Hemmings and was surprised at this as he habitually knocked Hemmings up at 4.30 am each morning for work. Mr Bradshaw subsequently went downstairs and knocked on the Hemmings' door. When he got no reply he opened it and entered the room. He was faced with a blood-besmeared carpet and bed linen and immediately realized something was amiss. He summoned the other lodgers and instructed them to fetch the police. Mr Bradshaw then set off for work.

Police Constable Cole, who lived nearby, was the first to be informed. He sent for help. Sergeant Dempster was quickly at the scene. When a woman's blood-soaked body was discovered, Dr Scott of Woodhouse was summoned. On examining the body, Dr Scott was quick to confirm what the police officers already suspected: that the woman's wounds were not self-inflicted. Sergeant Dempster sent word to Sheffield and a short time before nine o'clock, Superintendent Bielby arrived. He quickly took matters in hand and dispatched his officers in search of Edward Hemmings.

Superintendent Bielby remained at the murder scene and, after viewing the body, conducted a thorough examination of the room. He discovered a partially burned razor in the fire grate and the remains of some clogs. These clogs had been a bone of contention to Hemmings, who had shown them to his landlady the week before, after they had split, which had given him an excuse to return home early from work. He had told her that he was tired of life and did not care how soon it was ended. This led the police to suppose that Hemmings might commit suicide.

It was later found that an axe was missing from the kitchen and it was believed that the axe and the razor already discovered were the murder weapons. The axe was discovered later in the day in a sump near Woodhouse Junction Station. In the Hemmings' room were found carefully preserved books, which Ted Hemmings had gained as Sunday school prizes. Scripture texts adorned the walls. Documents were discovered revealing the Hemmings' had obtained furniture on hire from Mr Bailey of Rotherham and from Mr A.H. Banner of Attercliffe Road, Sheffield. There were also arrears owed on a sewing machine obtained from the Bradbury Machine Company, Wakefield. Another document showed that Hemmings was in arrears for a joint life insurance policy on himself and his wife with the Prudential Insurance Company. He owed them 4s 2d; the amount being payable on the policy was £25 12s.

A description of the suspected murderer was released. Edward Hemmings stood approximately 5 feet 6 inches tall. He was stoutly built, had black hair, a thick dark moustache and broad face. He was dressed in heavy moleskin trousers, black worsted jacket and vest and wore a light-brown cap with peak front and a pair of old laced boots.

It was ascertained that Ted Hemmings had been seen leaving the house at 4.00 am by a man named Hill, who was on his way to work. Mr Hill had followed him as far as Woodhouse Junction Station. There were no reported sightings after that. There were speculations in various newspapers that Hemmings had committed suicide but this was not the case. On leaving Woodhouse, Hemmings had headed for Doncaster. Arriving after dark he presented himself at the Guildhall, saying that he was a vagrant. They gave him a ticket, which procured him a bed in the workhouse. Next morning he walked to Featherstone, where he went to the house of someone he knew named Fox. The door was opened by the man's wife and she invited him in. Mrs Fox knew of the murder and expressed her surprise at seeing Hemmings alive and told him she thought he would have drowned himself, to which Hemmings replied he thought too much about himself to do that. Mrs Fox made Hemmings a cup of tea and gave him something to eat. Afterwards he had a wash, and then set out for his parents' house. He had a change of heart as he got within a mile or so of their house and decided not to cause his mother any further grief. He headed for Normanton Police Station, where he gave himself up. When he was searched he was found to be without means, his only possession being a miners' union card. Hemmings was curious to know if the hangman would get his clothes, a question he repeatedly asked the police officers. In the early hours of the following morning, Saturday, 18 February, he was taken by train to Sheffield, where he arrived at 4.00 am, from whence he was taken by foot to the West Riding Police Station in Burngreave Road.

Meanwhile, the inquest had opened on Friday, 17 February, before coroner Dossey Wightman, Esquire, at the Junction Hotel, Woodhouse. Having taken evidence of identification of the dead woman, the coroner, before adjourning the proceedings until the following Wednesday, issued a burial certificate.

The *Sheffield and Rotherham Independent* newspaper reported on Tuesday, 21 February:

> When it was known that the unfortunate young woman, in addition to being the victim of a brutal murder, was to be interred in a parish coffin at the expense of the parish authorities, the people of Woodhouse were much exercised, and a public subscription was soon got up for the purpose of assisting the relatives to procure for the deceased what is so dear in the hearts of those in the humbler ranks of life – a 'decent burial'. While the parish found the coffin and paid for the grave, the funds collected sufficed to put a little stain on the former [an unadorned, unstained pine or deal parish coffin] and to ornament it with metal handles and a breastplate. The body had remained in the room where the murder was committed in Furnace Lane, and the coffin arrived about one o'clock yesterday, the appearance of which caused a small crowd to collect near. The body was then put into the coffin and the lid screwed down … At three o'clock the cortège started from the house. No hearse or other vehicle was used, the coffin being carried shoulder

high to the cemetery, which is at least a mile and a half distant, and uphill most of the way. The bearers numbered twelve, and they carried the coffin in sets of four. Three policemen headed the procession, then came the coffin (which was not covered with a pall), and the bearers, with the mourners coming behind. None of the relatives of the husband were present.

The inquest was resumed on Wednesday, 22 February. George Bradshaw, a railway labourer, said that he lodged in Furnace Lane, Woodhouse, in a house owned by Charles Everitt Kennington and his wife, along with two other men and Ted and Annie Hemmings, who had occupied a room on the ground floor for about five weeks. He said he had last seen Mrs Hemmings alive at about 9.30 pm the previous night when they were chatting in the kitchen, during which time Ted Hemmings was sitting alone in their room. The kitchen was used as a sort of living room by all the lodgers. Mr Bradshaw said his own room was immediately above the Hemmings'. He said at about 2.45 am on 15 February he heard what he described as a bit of a screech coming from the Hemmings' room. He got out of bed and shouted down the stairs, 'Ted, Ted, what's amiss?'

To which, Hemmings replied, 'Nowt.'

Mr Bradshaw added that he knew that the noise had been made by Mrs Hemmings, because she had made the noise before when in fits. Mr Bradshaw then went back to bed.

The coroner: 'You said something about fits. Do you know that the deceased woman was subject to fits?'

Bradshaw: 'Yes.'

The coroner: 'You have seen her in them?'

Bradshaw: 'Yes, and have been with her at the time.'

The coroner: 'Has she ever screamed in them?'

Bradshaw: 'Yes.'

The coroner: 'You say you thought she was in a fit?'

Bradshaw: 'Yes, it is just what I did think, and nothing else.'

The coroner: 'What did you hear next?'

Bradshaw: 'I heard Hemmings go out about four o'clock.'

The coroner: 'Was this his usual time for going out?'

Bradshaw: 'No, Sir; I should think about half-past four reckoned to be his usual time.'

The coroner: 'What did you see or hear then?'

Bradshaw: 'I got up about five o'clock, and went down. I shook Hemmings' door and shouted.'

The coroner: 'Did you get any reply?'

Bradshaw: 'No; I heard nothing.'

The coroner: 'What then?'

Bradshaw: 'I knocked again at the door and, hearing nothing, opened the door.'

The coroner: 'What did you see?'

Bradshaw: 'I saw blood on the clothes which were covered over her.'

The coroner: 'Did you not see any body?'

Bradshaw: 'No. I shouted, and the others came up.'

The coroner: 'Before you did anything else?'

Bradshaw: 'Yes.'

The coroner: 'Who came?'

Bradshaw: 'The two men who were lodging there, Fred Ravendale and Benjamin Rowley. When they came I sent for the police.'

The coroner: 'Didn't you see the woman at all?'

Bradshaw: 'No, Sir.'

The coroner: 'Did you send for the police before you saw the woman at all?'

Bradshaw: 'Yes.'

The coroner: 'At that time you had not seen the deceased, the bed clothes were over her?'

Bradshaw: 'Yes, she was covered from head to foot. I saw nothing at all of her; I only saw the blood. I believed she was there, but I could not see her.'

The coroner: 'Did you see any more of it, or did you go away?'

Bradshaw: 'I saw no more, and I went away to work.'

The coroner: 'Had you heard any quarrel before then?'

Bradshaw: 'No, not a word.'

The coroner: 'Never before?'

Bradshaw: 'No; at no time.'

The coroner: 'You have never known Hemmings and his wife quarrel?'

Bradshaw: 'No.'

The coroner: 'Did you see any razors or knives?'

Bradshaw: 'No, Sir; I saw nothing.'

Arthur William Scott, the surgeon practising at Woodhouse, said he was called to the scene of the murder at half-past six in the morning. When he went to the house he was directed to a bedroom on the ground floor where he saw a woman's head and blood on the bedclothes, and also a large quantity of blood on the floor. He turned the bedclothes down and saw the body of the deceased. She was quite dead and appeared to have been in that condition for more than three hours. Rigor mortis had set in. Mr Scott said he found that the woman's throat had been cut from ear to ear, which probably caused the blood on the floor. There was also an incised wound above the left eye, which had fractured the skull and exposed the brain to view. He said that this wound had probably caused the blood on the bed-clothes. Mr Scott was of the opinion that the wound on the head had been inflicted first and that it would cause the victim to have become insensible. He did not think it necessary to open the body, the cause of death clearly being the cut to the throat. The windpipe and gullet were completely divided, and the spine laid bare. Mr Scott added that the wound gaped 8 or 10 inches and would have caused instant death. The victim might have lived a few hours after the blow to the head had the throat not been cut. He found the two middle fingers and the thumb on the left hand were nearly severed, the cuts being made on the inside, as if Mrs Hemmings had seized a knife or sharp instrument and it had been drawn sharply out of her closed hand. There was also a cut on the right cheek and a small cut to another part of the neck. The body was lying with the head towards the fireplace and resting upon the left arm and was dressed only in night apparel. Mr Scott said he was in the room when a razor blade was found by Superintendent Bielby in the fireplace. He added that he had formed the opinion that the wound to the head had been caused by a hatchet, and the hatchet produced at the inquest was likely to have caused the injury. The blade exactly corresponded with the wound.

Other witnesses corroborated the events leading up to the murder, at the end of which, in addressing the jury, the coroner said they had to say who in their opinion committed the murder. He then added:

The doctor said the wounds could not possibly have been self-inflicted. The question then arose, 'Who did it?' There could not be very much doubt about that if the evidence was worth anything at all. So far as I know there are no suspicions against any other person whatsoever with the exception of Edward Hemmings, her husband, who, it has been proved, had used threats that he would 'finish' her for some reason or other. She had been found 'finished'. Edward Hemmings absconded and this, of course, has always an ugly look. If anyone else had murdered the woman there would be no reason why he should have absconded . . .

The jury, after a few minutes' deliberation, returned a verdict of 'wilful murder' against Edward Hemmings; he was committed to take his trial at the next assizes.

On Friday, 24 February, Hemmings came up before West Riding magistrates, Alderman Michael Hunter and Mr T.W. Cadman, for a preliminary examination at Sheffield Town Hall. As the court was adjourning for lunch, Annie Hemmings' eldest sister, Anice Jones, got up from her seat and went over to the prisoner. Before either the police or court officials could intervene the following exchange was heard to take place between them. Weeping bitterly, Anice said to her brother-in-law, 'I am sorry it has come to this. If you had taken my advice it would not have happened. Speak the truth, Ted.'

For the first time since his arrest, Hemmings broke down and, holding out his hand to Anice, said, 'Well, I confess I have done it.'

At the close of the day's proceedings, when asked if he had anything to say, Hemmings said he had nothing to say and confirmed when asked that he wished to reserve his defence. The prisoner was then formally committed to take his trial at the next assizes commencing on 10 March.

Hemmings was tried at Leeds Assizes on Wednesday, 15 March, before Mr Justice Bruce. Mr Cyril Dodd QC, MP and Mr Arthur Bairstow prosecuted, and Mr Walter Beverley defended. The trial opened at 10.30 am and concluded at 6.00 pm. The gallery was filled to capacity; many spectators were men and women who knew either the murdered woman or the prisoner and who had made their way to Leeds from Normanton. Hemmings had intended to conduct his own defence. However, some of his friends got together and raised the money to pay for the services of Bradford barrister Walter Beverley, briefed by a solicitor from Wakefield, Edward Lodge. It seems that despite Hemmings having said he would go to the scaffold like a man, he was now determined to dodge that fatal journey if it could be avoided. On 16 March, the *Sheffield and Rotherham Independent* reported that the defence had:

> ... got up as effective a defence as was possible under the circumstances. Immediately after the judge had taken his seat, Hemmings was placed in the dock. He walked with a firm, almost a defiant, step. His face was a little paler than on his last appearance in public, and his hitherto clean-shaven chin showed a growth of reddish beard. But his three weeks' detention at Wakefield had wrought no perceptible change in his demeanour. At no stage in the trial did he appear to be impressed with the gravity of his position, and but for the fact that he several times prompted his counsel or his solicitor – proving that he was intelligently following the evidence, and understood the advantage of making a point which would tell in his favour – a stranger might have supposed that he was merely an interested spectator in what was going on ... As time went on the prisoner became somewhat fidgety, but not so much as might have been expected, having regard to the length of the trial.

In his opening speech for the prosecution Mr Cyril Dodd said:

> It is my intention to lay before the jury a résumé of the evidence in simple language and to endeavour to avoid any unnecessary comment. The prisoner was a collier, who at the time of the death of his wife, was lodging with her at the house of a railway porter named Kennington, in Furnace Lane, Woodhouse, Sheffield. They had been lodging there for five weeks, and, so far as we know, got on comfortably there. They occupied one room on the ground floor of the house, and they were seen in this room about nine-thirty o'clock on the night before the 16th February, by the

landlady. The deceased was then preparing food for her husband to take with him to work the next day. The landlady [Mrs Eliza Kennington] said they seemed on very good terms at that time.

Mr Dodd went on to outline George Bradshaw's version of events and then went on to describe the scene of the murder:

The dead body of the deceased was found lying on the floor of the bedroom, the skull being fractured, and the throat cut from ear to ear. The body was covered over with a sheet. There were cuts on the fingers of one of the deceased's hands, which indicated that she had struggled with her murderer. A large quantity of blood was found on the floor, on the stockings of the deceased, as if she had trodden in it, and on the clothes. Apparently she had been dealt a blow on the forehead with an axe, and her throat cut by a razor. A razor was found in the fire. An axe was missed from its usual place in the kitchen, and subsequently found in a gully a short distance away from Woodhouse. It appeared that after leaving the house the prisoner wandered to Normanton, where his friends lived, and where he was married, his wife having been in service there. He supposed under similar circumstances men did wander, mechanically, to places with which they had been familiar before. He went to the house of a Mrs [Charlotte] Fox, near Normanton, where he once lodged. Mrs Fox had heard of the murder and his supposed connection with it, and also broached the subject to him. He said he left his wife's body on the rug on the floor, and covered it with a cloth, and that he was wearing a cap that belonged to his wife, which he brought away because he wanted something belonging to her. He then said he loved the ground his wife trod on. Being asked why he had come back to Normanton, he replied that he wanted to see the old folks once again. Mrs Fox remarked that she would drown herself if she were in his position. In answer to that the prisoner said he had felt a weight upon his mind for several weeks, but now he felt as light as a feather. The next that was heard of the prisoner was that he gave himself up to Inspector Turton and Sergeant Ford at Normanton Police Station. He seemed to have had a conversation with the officers, to whom he admitted having killed his wife, but said he did not regret it, and announced his intention of going to the scaffold like a man. When he was handed over to Superintendent Bielby at Sheffield and charged with murder he said, 'It's right.' The evidence will show that the prisoner had carried about with him a razor. I think the jury will have no difficulty in coming to the conclusion that the deceased was killed by the prisoner, and then comes the question – an important one but always a difficult one in such cases, to determine why he did it. What was the motive that actuated the prisoner in committing this crime? It is impossible to find for any crime of this gravity an adequate motive, at any rate which could operate upon the mind of a reasonable man and induce him to commit wilful murder ... The deceased woman seems to have had a strong desire to have a house of her own, and not to live in lodgings, while he [the prisoner] seemed to have felt somewhat his inability to satisfy her by giving her a cottage such as she wanted. Some of the witnesses will show that the couple had changed their residence several times since they were married, while more than once they parted and came together again and lived fairly comfortably. It also appears from the evidence that the prisoner with or without reason was jealous, first of one lodger and then of another, so that their married life could not have been absolutely happy. There is evidence to show that the prisoner had talked of taking his wife's life some time before the crime was committed, and he showed a razor he had bought.

In concluding his opening speech, Mr Dodd told the hushed courtroom:

The witnesses included several relatives of the deceased; and are mainly in a humble station in life. When the jury have heard their evidence I am sure that the jury will be convinced that they are people who have come into court with the intention of giving an accurate narrative of what they saw and knew. I submit that it will be impossible after the evidence has been heard, to doubt that the deceased has been the victim of a murder of a deliberate character, and that the prisoner is guilty of the crime.

The court heard much the same evidence as was given at the inquest and during the committal proceedings.

Having heard all the evidence Mr Beverley addressed the jury on behalf of the prisoner:

I feel very keenly the weight of responsibility that rests upon me in defending this man. My responsibility, however, is nothing compared to that of you, the jury, for according to what your verdict might be this unhappy man will either live or die. To kill is one thing; to commit murder is an entirely different kind of thing. That the prisoner killed his wife you can have no doubt but the question is did he kill her with malice of forethought? Did he premeditate the act? I invite you to bring in a verdict of manslaughter, an offence varying greatly in degree and one for which it is competent for his Lordship to commit to penal servitude for life. The prisoner has been shown to be of irreproachable character. He was well known in Normanton for some years, and all his acquaintances gave him a good name. Then he got married, and the marriage almost turned out to be his death warrant. A more ill-assorted union could not well have been entered into. He was of a jealous turn of mind, who loved his wife fondly, and would often coax her when he was in a temper. The wife was quick-tempered and often defied her husband, telling him she should do just as she liked and take her own course. When the husband complained to Kelly [a male relative of whom Hemmings had become jealous] of his conduct and that of the deceased, the latter never resented it, but told her husband it served him right. She had frequently said she did not care for him. I think you will not fail to infer from the evidence that the deceased was not quite the wife she ought to have been to the prisoner. Many circumstances have been mentioned to show that the prisoner was very fond of his wife. Even the night before the murder he was seen bending over his wife in an affectionate attitude, while she was knitting – spooning in fact [indulging in demonstrative love-making]. That was not the conduct of a man who had a preconceived notion of destroying his wife's life. If he had premeditated such a crime he had plenty of opportunities of carrying it out during the time they lodged at the Kenningtons'. I ask you, gentlemen of the jury, to believe that the prisoner was not serious when he uttered the threats. As to the razor, he was in the habit of using it, and it did not appear that he bought it for the purpose of murder. On the night before the murder the deceased was in the kitchen laughing and joking with the lodgers, while the prisoner was probably brooding over the old sore. I ask you to put yourselves in the place of this man, then perhaps you will be able to appreciate the amount of provocation the man felt. No doubt he had got into a frame of mind that made him susceptible to wrong motives, and one can understand how the lively spirit of his wife would be calculated to increase his anger. There was the occasion when the prisoner heard the deceased using severe language towards herself.

It was at this point that Mr Justice Bruce interrupted the defence's closing speech to appraise the jury on a point of law, saying, 'Gentlemen of the jury, I must impress upon you that no words, however opprobrious, could be considered in law provocation sufficient to reduce homicide to manslaughter, if the killing was effected by a deadly weapon.'

Mr Beverley suggested that it might be otherwise in exceptional circumstances. To which his Lordship replied, 'I am compelled to advise the jury according to the opinion I have expressed.'

Mr Beverley made a final attempt to try to sway the jury in his client's favour by suggesting that Hemmings might have received greater provocation. He suggested that weapons might have been used by the deceased. He said there was no evidence to the contrary and there was no knowing what took place in the bedroom on that fatal morning.

The judge was once again prompted to interrupt the defence by pointing out, 'Every homicide is deemed in law to be murder unless evidence is given to show it was otherwise.'

Mr Beverley continued by contending that express malice had not been proved. He said there might have been a serious quarrel in the bedroom, and in the heat of the moment the prisoner might have snatched up the weapon that was nearest to hand and struck his wife. Mr Beverley concluded by saying,

'All afternoon I have been endeavouring to save a drowning man, and I ask you, gentlemen of the jury, to assist me; and to supply any deficiency of which I might have been guilty in conducting this case on behalf of the prisoner.'

His speech now over and the case for the defence being complete, the learned counsel resumed his seat. As he did so the courtroom erupted in spontaneous applause. It was now time for the judge to take over the proceedings. In his summing up, Mr Justice Bruce told the jury:

> You have a serious and heavy duty to perform. You have to do justice to the prisoner and perform the duty imposed upon you by the State to give a verdict according to the evidence. If you are satisfied that according to the evidence, the prisoner is guilty of wilful murder, I am sure, however painful that duty might be, you will bring a verdict of guilty. A good deal has been said by the learned counsel who so ably defended the prisoner about the absence of evidence of express malice. But in law every man has to take the consequences of his own acts. When a man strikes his wife or any other person on the head with a deadly weapon, from the very act itself there is, in the eye of the law, malice. The law implied malice to a man who shoots at another man with a pistol, or stabs at him with a knife. It is not for you to seek evidence of expressed malice. You have to consider whether what was done was done under such circumstances of provocation it would justify the act, if a man killed another in self-defence it was no crime; if done under great provocation the act was not justifiable, but the crime might be reduced to the minor one of manslaughter. It is highly improbable that this woman's death was caused by a person in a momentary fit of passion caused by provocation. Even if there were provocation by words – and that was not proved – mere words of reproach, however grievous, is not sufficient provocation to reduce homicide to manslaughter, if effected by deadly weapons. In the present case there was not merely the blow on the head, but the terrible gash on the throat. The poor woman did not die with but one mark upon her body. I do not think all this could have been done in a momentary passion produced by

provocation of words. The prisoner, in his numerous con-
versations, has not said his wife provoked him. He never
made any suggestion that his wife made an attack upon
him. His only suggestion was as to certain words she had
used about him in Mrs Kennington's kitchen, and that took
place some considerable time before the prisoner killed her.
You can have no doubt how the deceased came by her
death and who killed her, and there is no evidence of sufficient provocation to reduce the crime to manslaughter. It
is my duty to tell you that the words the deceased woman
had used are not sufficient for that purpose.

The jury, having listened to the judge's summing up, retired.
After discussing the evidence they returned after thirty-five
minutes and delivered their verdict. They found the prisoner
was 'guilty of the wilful murder of his wife' but they recommended him to mercy. The Clerk of Arraigns then rose and
asked if the prisoner had anything to say why sentence of death
should not be passed, to which Hemmings replied that he
would like to make a few remarks. He then launched into a long
rambling speech in which he cited incidents pertaining to his
jealousy concerning his wife's association with various relatives
and friends. The speech made little sense to the spectators and
at one point Hemmings broke down before continuing. He
paused for breath and the judge, clearly thinking Hemmings
had finished, began to pronounce sentence, at which point
Hemmings attempted to continue with his speech. On being
told he could not do so by an official, he acquiesced; although it
was clear he still had more to say.

Mr Justice Bruce then addressed the prisoner in the dock:

After a most careful trial, and after listening with attention
to the most able defence delivered by your counsel, the jury
have found you guilty of the crime of murder. They have
also recommended you to mercy, and in reference to that all
I can say is that it shall be forwarded to the proper quarter.
The evidence given in the court today proves that you have
been guilty of a most cruel and brutal murder. You have
with heartless violence taken the life of a woman whom you
were bound by every obligation to succour and protect.
You sent her without warning to eternity. You will have an

opportunity of preparation, which you denied her. Let me implore you eagerly to embrace the opportunities of spiritual consolation which will be offered to you in prison.

The judge then pronounced sentence of death on the prisoner.

The jury's recommendation for mercy was ignored. Various newspapers, including the *Sheffield and Rotherham Independent*, reported on Saturday, 1 April that Hemmings' solicitor, Mr Edward Lodge, had received news from the Home Secretary, Mr Asquith, that he would not accede to the petition for a reprieve and that the law must take its course. On Monday, 3 April, Hemmings was visited in the condemned cell at Armley Gaol, Leeds, by his parents, Emmanuel and Sarah Hemmings, his brother, Thomas, his sister, Sarah and his brother-in-law, John Baker. They remained with him for twenty minutes. Hemmings' seventy-three-year-old father left Armley with his family; from the look on his face it was evident that the thought of his son's fate had told upon him considerably. Later in the day, James Billington, the executioner, arrived at Armley from Bolton, for his overnight stay. The following morning at 8.00 am, Edward Hemmings was hanged in the permanent execution shed adjoining the cookhouse. Billington gave him a drop of 7 feet 5 inches. Death was instantaneous. Forty seconds after the clock had struck eight, the black flag was hoisted.

On Thursday, 6 April, a letter was published in the *Sheffield and Rotherham Independent*. It was written by Edward Hemmings in the condemned cell at Armley Gaol and sent to Thomas Cressy, of Normanton Common. Part of the letter is transcribed here:

If ever there was a man tried to do what was right and tried all as ever he knew how to live a Christian's life, I tried to live one, but, alas! there came a time when I was doing no work. I was living with Mrs Fox, but we flitted with them and went to Sourbrigg, Featherstone Common, they call it. Well, what with doing no work, and running into debt at my lodgings, I seemed to grow colder and colder, and to stop away from meeting[s], and at last I stopped going altogether. One day I stood against Birch's grocer's shop. And a young man came by – an old companion – and begged of me to go and have a drink, and doing no work, and running my board money on, and to tell you the truth I seemed miserable. What with one thing and what with another I yielded, and I am sorry to say I stopped and got drunk . . . I have a favour to ask. The first Sunday night after you get this can you arrange that you take to your text 'What shall it profit man though he gain the whole world and lose his own soul', or 'What would a man give in exchange for his soul'. I forget which chapter but I dare say you will know where to look for it . . . When I committed the murder, even a minute or two after it was done, I would freely have given 10,000 worlds if but then in my possession. But it was too late. The truth was not spoken at the trial, and I shall be able to prove it when we come to stand before the judgement bar of God. I am pleased to know this – that when we appear before our Maker to give an account of the deeds done in this body, thank God the truth will have to be told up there . . .

From
Edward Hemmings
Armley Gaol

# CHAPTER 9

# Murder at Christmas Time 1905

*... while she was trying to escape from her attacker, knocked down by the broom, which had then been wielded with enormous force to cause massive internal injuries ...*

On Saturday, 23 December 1905, Police Constable Winfield was on duty in West Bar Green, when he was approached by a man, whose bearing and demeanour led the constable to believe he was somewhat the worse for drink. The man, who later identified himself as Harry Walters, said to Constable Winfield, 'I want you to come with me.'

To which request Constable Winfield asked, 'What's the matter?'

Winfield then told the constable, 'I have been out drinking and came home and found my wife laid on her back with no clothes on and blood coming from her. I don't know how it happened and I thought it my place to come and report the matter to you.'

Constable Winfield then followed the drunken man to No. 7 house, Court 12, Upper Allen Street. It was an abysmal abode but not untypical of the many enclaves of such slum dwellings that pock-marked large areas of Sheffield in the early twentieth century.

On arriving at Court 12, and having entered Walters' house, Constable Winfield was immediately confronted by a horrendous sight; the room was in disarray and there was much blood apparent. A woman was lying on the floor clad only in a flimsy garment to the upper body but, apart from her wearing shoes and stockings, she was, as Walters had told Constable Winfield, otherwise naked. Lying near the woman's body were a flat iron, ginger beer bottle and a blood-besmeared broom handle. Constable Winfield summoned help and police surgeon Dr Godfrey was sent for. While the surgeon was making his way to Court 12, the room in which the apparently lifeless woman's body lay was examined. Strewn across a chair and sofa were various items of female apparel, some of them bloodstained. A blood-smeared piece of paper lay in the fireplace and blood was spattered on the floor, walls and first stair leading to the upper floor. There were signs that an unsuccessful attempt had been made to remove bloodstains from the floor. As the police looked around, Walters watched over them and stood swigging from a quart bottle of beer. As he was doing so, he uttered the words, 'My Poor Sal Willey. If she's dead, I'll be dead. I gave her a sovereign this afternoon and we have been drinking. I can't do anything with her when she's been drinking. We have had a bit of a quarrel but that's nothing. I fetched you like a man.'

When Dr Godfrey arrived, following only a brief examination of the woman's body he quickly ascertained that death had indeed taken place but only recently, as the body was still warm. The body was conveyed to the mortuary by fire brigade ambulance. By this time, other officers, including the deputy chief constable, had arrived at the scene. On being told he was to be arrested on a charge of murder and taken to the Central Police Office, Walters replied, 'I am not guilty.'

Following him being taken into custody, on being searched, he had half a crown, one shilling and two halfpennies on his person. There was blood on his clothing and on his boots, which had been washed. The police investigation was soon underway ;and it was quickly established that no one in the vicinity had heard any sounds of quarrelling, fighting, or, indeed, any commotion whatsoever. It was also revealed that there had been visitors that very afternoon to No. 7 house.

It was soon established that at 5.00 pm Mrs Bradshaw, who was an assistant rent collector, called and her knock was answered by Walters. On being asked if the missus was in, he replied that she was not. Just a few minutes later there was another caller at No. 7 house, when fish vendor Margaret Revill came to ask for 6½d to pay for fish. On hearing her knock, Walters called, 'Come in, if you're a woman.'

On being told she was a fish wife and what was the purpose of her visit, Walters said, 'She's upstairs. Call her down.'

Having done so, Margaret Revill watched as Sarah Walters came downstairs, her clothes in disarray and according to Revill appeared as if she had been fighting. Sarah said to her husband, 'Pay her.'

Walters, who was reclining on the sofa, pulled out 5½d from his pocket, saying, 'That's all I've got.'

He then became agitated and said there was 3s 6d missing from one of his pockets and a five shilling piece missing from the other and accused his wife of taking it. Margaret Revill said the woman, who appeared to be rather the worse for drink (although she added the man was even more drunk), ignored Walters and, turning away from him, said to her, 'Never mind lass, come in the morning. It's Good Sunday. I'll pay thee then.'

Harry Walters said somewhat brusquely, 'As soon as you've gone, I'll kill her stone dead if she does not find the money.'

Realizing that her money would not be forthcoming, Margaret Revill left. Around 5.30 pm, rent collector Annie Drakard called at No. 7 to see if she could achieve what her assistant had not, the successful collection of the due rent. Having received no reply to her knock, she pushed open the door. She saw Sarah Walters in a pitiful state laying dead on the floor. She fetched Emily Bradshaw and the two women, having taken a closer look at the body, draped a skirt over it for the sake of decency. Within minutes of the two women leaving, a neighbour, twelve-year-old Margaret Osbourne, was sent to No. 7 house to collect 1½d, which her mother was owed. The door was ajar and she pushed it open, while saying at the same time, 'If you please, missus, will you send mamma that three half-pence?'

The girl was startled to see Mrs Walters lying on her back, with her knees drawn up, and a pool of blood nearby. She appeared to be naked but had a skirt thrown over her knees; and there was a man standing over her. Margaret took to her heels and ran home and told her father what she had seen, to which the girl received the reply, 'Don't come here with any of your romancing tales.'

At around the same time the girl was making her report to her father, Harry Walters was knocking on the door of his neighbour, Ann Austwick. He said to her, 'Will you come to my wife? I believe she is dead.'

Walters then went to find a constable and after a few minutes, happened upon Constable Winfield.

Harry Walters met Susan McConnell in Wakefield in the autumn of 1905. Until October that year she had been living in Sutton-in-Ashfield with her husband, whom she had married three-and-a-half years previously. She decided to leave him and eventually, after a series of unknown adventures, ended up in a public house in Wakefield, where she made the acquaintance of Harry Walters, an encounter that was within only a matter of weeks to prove fatal. She called herself Mrs Jackson. Both she and Walters were prone to heavy drinking, She, at forty-three years old, was five years his senior. For the sake of convenience and propriety, Harry Walters took to referring to Sarah McConnell, alias Mrs Jackson, as his wife. Before they moved to Upper Allen Street, they lived together at Barnsley, then Darnall. Walters found work at Orgreave Colliery.

On 27 December, Walters was brought before Sheffield stipendiary magistrate, Edward M.E. Welby. During the course of the proceedings it was revealed that the deceased had bruising to her spine and knees, a large bruise on her right arm, bruising to her right hip, in addition to scratches to her face and upper lip, notwithstanding the appalling injuries that were ultimately to have resulted in her death, which had been caused by an implement (believed to have been the blood-besmeared broom handle) being rammed up her vagina and rupturing her internal organs; the cause of death ultimately being shock and haemorrhaging.

On 28 December, the inquest was opened by Dossey Wightman, Esquire, at the Public Mortuary in Plum Lane, Corporation Street. The deceased's brother, Arthur Wiley, Margaret Revill, Elizabeth (Annie) Drakard, Ann Austwick, Police Constable Winfield and Dr Carter were all called to give evidence. Walters declined to give evidence himself and said, 'I'll reserve it while the court.'

On 4 January 1906, Walters appeared before Sheffield stipendiary magistrate, Edward Welby, Esquire. Mr Wing appeared for the prosecution and Sheffield solicitor Arthur Neal for the defence. That same day, the *Sheffield Telegraph* included in its report a description of the area where the murder had taken place:

> One of the many streets of mean unlovely homes which intersect the habited area, bounded on one side by St Phillips Road and on the other by Shalesmoor and West Bar Green. It is but five minutes' walk from one of the main arteries from the city to Hillsborough. Allen Street is, on the whole, one of the broadest best paved and most presentable of the uninviting thoroughfares in this district. It stretches from Shalesmoor across Meadow Street and on up the slope to St George's Church. But the dwellers in the houses abutting on the highways in this congested neighbourhood form merely a portion of the population. At the rear are courtyards with human dwellings grouped around them. The scene of the tragedy, No. 12 Court, is some distance up Allen Street between Well Meadow Street and Jericho Street. In relation to some of the courts in the city, No. 12 is by no means the worst. Reached by a slippery descending passage the court is perhaps 20 or 30 yards long and half that distance across. On either side of the slope are ten or a dozen little houses with a living room on the ground floor and sleeping accommodation upstairs, and No. 7 house is one of the row facing the entrance passage.

The same witnesses who had given evidence at the coroner's court gave evidence, at the conclusion of which, Mr Neal addressed the bench saying:

> No doubt an atrocious murder has been committed and the question was whether the prisoner was the person who had committed it. The evidence must excite suspicion. But his going to the next-door neighbour and asking her to come, his fetching a policeman, the open door and a number of other matters which I need not detail are quite inconsistent with this man being guilty of this crime. It was one of those cases in which the Prisoner's Evidence Act would be of supreme importance and he had thought it right to advise the prisoner that now was the proper time to give evidence.

When Walters was called to give his evidence he denied he had threatened the deceased when Mrs Revill was in the house and added that he had never threatened her in his life. He said he never quarrelled with her except on account of her drunkenness. He said that after Mrs Revill had left he had gone out and visited three public houses, The Black Man, in Scotland Street, the Lincoln Castle, in Edward Street and The Brocco Hotel, having a drink at each of them but meeting no one he knew. Remarkable, when one considers the timescale, but then he was a heavy drinker. Walters said how he had found the deceased when he got home. There was a skirt thrown over her. He described how he had put his arm under her head and tried to lift her up and called out her name but got no answer, which was when he got blood on his clothing; and how he had gone to neighbour Ann Austwick's house and then for the police. He also denied saying that money had been taken out of his pocket. Despite his denial of witnesses' evidence, he was committed for trial at the assizes.

Walters was tried before Mr Justice Walton on 23 March. John Strachan QC and Charles Lowenthal appeared for the Crown. Walters was defended by Harry T. Waddy and Victor Murray Coutts-Trotter. The medical evidence gave the prosecution's case great weight against Walters' version of events, although he maintained throughout that someone else had done the murder. The murdered woman's injuries suggested that she had first been assaulted, then most likely while she was trying to escape from her attacker, knocked down by the broom, which had then been wielded with enormous force to cause massive internal injuries. With regard to the amount of blood on the prisoner's clothing, particularly his boots, which although he had attempted to clean, were literally welting with blood, his clothing being so covered in blood, in keeping with the character of the crime, indicated he could not possibly have obtained such staining by merely lifting the woman's head as the prisoner had stated in his previous evidence. Witness evidence included testimony from Robert O'Neill, landlord of The Black Man, who denied Walters had been in his house on the afternoon of the murder. It also emerged that Walters had not been seen in the Lincoln Castle, where he had also said he had taken a drink. It was only David Holmes, of The Brocco Hotel who could confirm that his daughter, who was working in the bar on the afternoon in question, had served Walters at about 5.30 pm.

In his closing speech for the Crown, Mr Strachan emphasized the evidence concerning the amount of blood on the boots and said it was inconceivable that a stranger, having killed the deceased, would have then attempted to wash the blood up from the floor and increase the risk of being caught. For the defence, Mr Waddy submitted that the Crown's case depended entirely upon circumstantial evidence and closed by warning the jury against condemning a man upon such evidence. Mr Justice Walton was not convinced that the Crown had presented a strong enough case and in his summing up placed strong emphasis on an acquittal. His Lordship said there was no doubt that a terrible murder had been committed on the day in question, but it was important to make sure that the wrong man was not punished for it.

The jury retired for just thirty-five minutes. They found Harry Walters 'guilty of murder' but recommended him to mercy on the grounds of his drunken and incapable condition at the time. When the Clerk of Arraigns asked the prisoner if there was any reason why sentence of death should not be passed, Walters replied, 'I am not guilty. That's all.'

Sentence of death having duly been passed, Walters was taken back to Wakefield Prison. Arthur Neal quickly set about organizing an appeal, but this proved unsuccessful. Harry Walters was hanged by Henry Pierrepoint (assisted by his brother, Thomas) at Wakefield Prison on 10 April 1906, becoming the first prisoner to be hanged there.

# CHAPTER 10

# The Chinese Laundry Murder
# 1922

## *It was not long before a shovel struck something hard and the clank of metal was heard ...*

**S**ing Lee was already the successful owner of a Chinese Laundry in Liverpool, when in 1919 he opened his second such establishment at 231 Crookes Road, Sheffield. The building was a seven-roomed house with shop premises on the ground floor fronting the street. This new business proved popular and grew from strength to strength. By the summer of 1922, as well as various laundry staff, the shop also employed twenty-seven-year-old Lee Doon (also known as Leong Lun) and the shop manager, twenty-three-year-old Lily Siddall, who lived with her parents at 154 Forncett Street, Sheffield. The shop's owner, Sing Lee, had by this time become a familiar figure in the neighbourhood. He was highly regarded for his scrupulous honesty and his shop was noted for its particular cleanliness. Sheffield's small Chinese community looked up to Sing Lee as a man they could turn to should the need arise.

On Saturday, 9 September 1922, the shop was particularly busy. Miss Siddall did not leave the premises until 8.30 pm and as she said goodnight to Sing Lee, she left him in the company of Lee Doon. When she

*Sing Lee.* (Press Archive)

arrived at 11.30 am on Sunday morning to open the shop, she was confronted by Lee Doon, who was already up and about, which was not the usual occurrence, as both Sing Lee and Lee Doon generally slept in on a Sunday in the living quarters upstairs. When Sing Lee did not make his customary appearance, Miss Siddall asked Lee Doon where he was. The answer that he gave to her question startled Miss Siddall, to say the least, because when she asked where Sing Lee was, Lee Doon replied that he had gone away. Eager to know more, Miss Siddall pressed Lee Doon further. She asked him where he had gone. Then came the ominous reply, 'I do not know, I think he go back to China. This business belong to me now.'

Miss Siddall was not impressed by Lee Doon's explanation and thought it was a little odd. She had worked at the laundry since February and got on very well with Sing Lee, and found it difficult to believe that he would disappear like that without saying anything.

When Miss Siddall turned up for work on the following day she heard the sound of digging in the cellar. She enquired of Lee Doon if the landlord had sent some workmen but he told her it was none of her business. However, Miss Siddall's curiosity got the better of her and she was determined to find out exactly what was going on, so she went down into the cellar. There she was confronted by two men with picks and shovels. When she asked what they were doing she was told that Lee Doon had approached them on Sunday and told them he wanted a hole digging in the cellar, so that is what they were doing. Later in the day, Lee Doon went out, so in his absence Miss Siddall decided that a spot of amateur detective work was the order of the day. She went into the living quarters and entered Sing Lee's bedroom. In it, as well as his hat and attaché case, there were several other articles that Sing Lee habitually took with him when he went away on business. How very curious, she thought. Miss Siddall then went back downstairs and carried on with her normal duties.

When Miss Siddall arrived at the shop on Tuesday, Lee Doon told her that someone had fetched Sing Lee's trunk and taken it away in a taxi. As Lee Doon was telling Miss Siddall this latest piece of news, he was wearing a pair of Sing Lee's trousers. When asked why he was wearing them he said his own were dirty and were being washed. She also asked him why he was washing Sing Lee's bedding and why there was blood on one of the windows. Lee Doon replied, 'Bedding dirty. Blood from chicken.'

That afternoon, two parcels arrived addressed to Lee Doon. Judging by the contents it would appear that Lee Doon had decided to adopt a more proprietorial role, for the parcels contained a new hat and a shiny new pair of shoes. Later that afternoon, Lee Doon overstepped the mark with Miss Siddall by making a lascivious remark, which she greatly resented, and she showed her displeasure by pushing him away. Having offered her thirty shillings to look after the shop for the rest of the week, she told him to look after it himself. On Wednesday morning she went back to the shop and asked if there had been any communication from Sing Lee. When Lee Doon replied in the negative, Miss Siddall told him she would not be coming back to work until Sing Lee returned.

Thomas Marshall, living at 7 Toftwood Road, Crookes, was a particular friend of Sing Lee. On the Friday before Sing Lee's disappearance the two friends had made a tentative arrangement to go to the Hippodrome on Monday and, when he

*Sing Lee's Laundry, at 231 Crookes Road, Sheffield.* (Press Archive)

enquired of Lee Doon of the whereabouts of his friend, he was told that a telegram had arrived and Sing Lee had gone to London, taking £100 with him. Puzzled by this Mr Marshall returned to the shop later that evening. The shop door was locked but through the window he saw Lee Doon struggling with a trunk.

Miss Siddall continued to call in at the shop to see if there was any news of Sing Lee. She sent off a telegram to the shop in Prescott Road, Liverpool, to ask if Sing Lee had paid them a visit. A telegram came back saying that he had not visited them. On the Thursday, four days after Sing Lee's disappearance, Miss Siddall once again called in at the shop to enquire about Sing Lee. Lee Doon said, 'Don't think boss come back any more. Perhaps go to China. Perhaps go to Liverpool.'

Miss Siddall called on Sing Sai, a friend of Sing Lee, who lived in Barnsley Road, Crookes. By now she was deeply concerned and decided to go to Liverpool. There she spoke to Sing Lee's cousin, Sun Kwong Lee. She told him all that had occurred since the previous Sunday and he agreed to accompany her back to Sheffield. Shortly after their arrival in the early hours of Saturday morning they went immediately to the police. It was not long before a contingent of police had been dispatched to Crookes and they were soon at the laundry knocking on the shop door. When Lee Doon answered the door he was asked the whereabouts of Sing Lee, to which he replied he had gone away. An inspection of the cellar was requested.

The cellar was stocked with coal and coke and in all appearances everything seemed to be perfectly in order. It was only after some of the coal and coke had been removed that the obvious signs of recent digging became evident, as signs of the clay floor's disturbance was revealed. It was approaching daybreak when the officers began digging. Lee Doon remained perfectly calm and said nothing. It was not long before a shovel struck something hard and the clank of metal was heard. A metal trunk was soon revealed and this was dug out and carried upstairs. The trunk had a domed lid. It was 29½ inches long by 18 inches wide and 22 inches high. When it was opened it contained the body of Sing Lee. Lee Doon was immediately placed under arrest and removed from the premises. He said he didn't understand what was happening. When searched he was found to have £30 on him and he was also wearing a ring belonging to Sing Lee. It was established that two of the £5 notes contained within the £30 found on Lee Doon's person had been paid to Sing Lee during the week before his disappearance.

Police surgeon and university lecturer in forensic medicine, Dr Carter, arrived at the scene and examined the trunk and its contents. Sing Lee's body was laying on its back, tied with a rope, with its knees flexed and a running noose round the neck. The body was dressed in only singlet and drawers. There were gaping wounds to the head; one wound, which was very deep, extended from the ear to beneath the jaw. Inside the trunk were a bloodstained pillow and pillowcase.

The post-mortem examination revealed there were extensive fractures of the skull, including severe fractures at the base of the skull on the left side. The stomach contents revealed that the deceased had eaten a meal of rice and lentils about an hour and a half before he died. The injuries, which could not have been self-inflicted, had been caused by a blunt instrument. The bloodstained pillow and pillowcase were indicative that Sing Lee had been killed in bed. The cause of death was head injuries and haemorrhage.

Lee Doon was brought before Sheffield city magistrates at 10.30 am that morning. When asked if he understood English, the smartly dressed Chinaman shook his head. Lee Doon was remanded in custody until the following Friday. On Monday, 18 September, Coroner J. Kenyon Parker, Esquire, opened the inquest at the Nursery Street Coroner's Court. Language difficulties among witnesses resulted in an adjournment until 2.30 pm on Friday. Sing Lee's funeral took place on Thursday, 20 September. He was buried in a section of Anfield Cemetery, Liverpool, reserved for Chinese burials.

The resumed inquest took place the following day. Miss Siddall, Dr Carter and the officers who discovered the trunk gave their evidence and when Lee Doon was asked if he wished to give evidence – to the surprise of all concerned – he replied that he did. Despite having said before the magistrates that he didn't understand English, Lee Doon proved to have a good command of the language. He said:

> Sing Lee wrote to me in Manchester and asked me to come to Sheffield. I saw him taking morphia and I told him not to do it and he started fighting with me. We had a fight and I struck him. I found I had killed him. At the time I did not know the consequence. I was afraid and put him in the box. Then I took the box down to the cellar. I then engaged two men to dig a hole so that I could hide it and no one would be any the wiser. I covered the hole up ...

The coroner's jury returned a verdict of wilful murder. On the following day, Lee Doon was once again before the city magistrates. Sydney Robinson, Esquire, and J.W. Flint, Esquire, appeared for the Director of Public Prosecutions and Sheffield solicitor Keeble Hawson appeared for Lee Doon. Mr Flint commended Miss Siddall for her detective work. When asked if he wished to make a statement, Lee Doon said he wished to reserve his defence. He was committed to take his trial at the assizes.

Lee Doon was tried before Mr Justice Greer at Leeds Winter Gaol Delivery, on 1 December 1922. Mr W.J. Waugh KC, with Mr H.V. Rabaghati, appeared for the prosecution and Mr W.P. Donald for the defence. The main thrust of the case for the prosecution was that even if the two men had quarrelled, the amount of force used to inflict the injuries went far beyond anything necessary for Lee Doon's own defence; and the evidence of Dr Carter, the police surgeon, that Sing Lee had been killed in his bed seemed to negate any other claim. When Lee Doon went into the witness box, he said:

> On the Sunday after closing the shop at 9.00 pm I went into the drying room at the back of the house and lay on a sofa there. Sing Lee, after removing the silver from the till upstairs, came into the drying room and stood in front of the stove. He said, 'I wish I had an opium pipe so that I could have a smoke. It would be worth three shillings to have a smoke.' I asked him what he wanted to smoke opium for. I said, 'You have only £300 or £400 saved up and, if they get to know, you will be arrested. Lee replied his

smoking had nothing to do with him. He got vexed and made use of abusive language. I retorted by calling him a few names. He rolled up his sleeves and said he wanted to fight. He came for me and there was a fight and in the fight we fell to the ground, Lee striking his head on the stove. A flat iron fell from the stove and hit Lee on the head. Lee said that I was illegitimate and had no ancestors and it made me very angry. When I saw Lee was bleeding I wrapped his head up in two towels and took him back upstairs and put him on the bed. I put two pillows under him to raise him up, took his shirt and trousers off and covered him up with a blanket. I went for a drink for him and on my return I found him dead. I got frightened, saw the trunk and put him in it. He was too long for the trunk so I put one rope round his neck and the other round his feet to pull him together so that he would fit into the box. He had been dead an hour. I got frightened. I knew I should be held responsible for his death so I thought I would bury him. I washed up the blood.

Under cross-examination, the prisoner admitted that he had battered Sing Lee's head against the flat iron five or six times. Lee Doon then said, 'I took him by the armpits to get him upstairs. At that stage he had had the use of his legs.'

Dr Carter was recalled at this point and gave the opinion that he did not believe that Sing Lee would have been conscious after being struck with the iron and could not have taken any part in going up the stairs. In his closing speech for the defence, Mr Donald contended that the blows the accused struck were in self-defence and that it was not proved that when he struck them he intended either to kill or to cause grievous bodily harm to Sing Lee.

Mr Justice Greer, in his summing up, drew the jury's attention to the contradictory nature of Lee Doon's evidence. The jury returned a verdict of guilty and his Lordship duly donned the customary black cap and passed sentence of death. Lee Doon was hanged at Armley Gaol on 5 January 1923, by Thomas Pierrepoint.

# CHAPTER 11

# The Walkley Murder
# 1923

*I want you to go to 20 Lister Road –*
*I believe I have done Jack Clark in*
*with a hatchet, which I have thrown*
*away, probably in the chapel yard in*
*Walkley Road ...*

For most of his working life John William Eastwood earned his living as a chimney sweep. He married Ethel Gill in 1902. She ran her own buffing workshop in Sheffield and they had three children together, two of whom were christened John William and Ethel, after their parents. Arnold, the second of the Eastwood's children, had died at the age of three in 1910. At the time of their father's arrest for wilful murder on 29 July 1923, young John and Ethel were aged twenty and fourteen, respectively.

John (or Jack, as he was known by some) Eastwood had managed to evade service in the armed forces during the First World War, having been rejected by the army because he suffered from neurasthenia (a psychological disorder characterized by chronic fatigue and weakness). He did not work after 1915 and was, for some time, a patient at the Royal Infirmary. He was also treated for syphilis at Eccleshall Asylum in February 1915. The cumulative effects of these afflictions had given him the excuse to hang up his chimney sweep's brushes. Meanwhile, Ethel continued to run her buffing workshop very successfully. About eighteen months before the murder took place the Eastwoods had diversified and John had become the licensee of the Bay Horse Inn, situated at 72 Daniel Hill Street, Walkley, at its junction with Harworth Street, where they now lived. During his relatively short time as a publican he had developed a relationship with one of his customers, a young married woman named Mildred Parramore. He was then aged thirty-nine, she, twenty-two. Such was his infatuation with Mildred that they decided to run off together. They did so on 30 June 1923.

What seemed like a good idea clearly turned out otherwise and by 12 July, John and Mildred were both back in Sheffield. Mildred's husband was happy to have her back but Ethel refused her husband not only her bed but also her roof. From that point onwards, Eastwood, having relinquished the running of the Bay Horse Inn to the care of Ethel when he left her for a younger woman, she now refused to even speak to him. Eastwood was left with no choice but to find a bed wherever he could.

One of the casual staff at the inn was forty-eight-year-old John Joseph Clark, who helped out as barman and potman. He worked in the cutlery industry as a spoon and fork stamper but he was also experienced in the licensing trade, having at one time been steward, with his wife Eva as stewardess, of the Institute of the Antediluvian Order of Buffaloes, in West Street. John Clark was himself an enthusiastic Buffalo. He had helped out at the Bay Horse Inn for a long time. He and Eva lived with their two sons, Jack, aged eighteen, and Harry, aged ten, and Clark's seventy-four-year-old father, in Lister Road. Eastwood and Clark got on well together and Eastwood asked Clark to put in a good word with Ethel for him, in the hope that she would take him back. When Clark's pleas on Eastwood's behalf did not work, Eastwood made something of a nuisance of himself by turning up in the evenings at the inn for a drink. He had been sleeping at various addresses since his return from Liverpool, including the home of Mr and Mrs Arthur Hilton at No. 1 Court, 8 Greaves Street, from which address he had been scraping a living by resuming his old trade as a chimney sweep. Eastwood had also slept on the couch at the home of John and Eva Clark at 20 Lister Road. On several occasions he had refused to leave the inn at the end of his drinking session and it had been necessary for Ethel to call the police to persuade him to leave. During his absence in Liverpool, Ethel had applied to have the licence of the Bay Horse Inn transferred to her, which was ratified by the magistrates at the transfer sessions on

Wednesday, 26 July. When John Eastwood went to the inn that evening, he was confronted by the name Ethel Eastwood painted above the doorway, displaying to all that his tenure as licensee was over and he was now officially an ex-publican.

Although John Clark and his wife were very happily married, Eastwood had somehow got it into his head that during his absence in Liverpool, Clark and his own wife, Ethel, had forged an attachment. A far as anyone could tell there was nothing amiss between Eastwood and Clark, indeed, as the *Sheffield and Rotherham Daily Independent* reported on Monday, 30 July:

> Eastwood and Clark met continuously, and were quite amiable to each other, and they chatted together at Saturday dinnertime. On Saturday night Mrs Eastwood stated her husband came to the inn and he was quite sober, one of his drinks being a 'lemon dash'. He asked to stay the night, and when this was refused he showed a strong disinclination to leave at closing time. Eventually he left reluctantly, after quite peaceful persuasion . . .

At 1.30 am on Sunday morning, John and Eva Clark were asleep in bed at their home in Lister Road. Mrs Clark was awakened by someone throwing pebbles at the window. She looked out and saw it was Eastwood. Thinking he wanted somewhere to sleep for the night she roused her husband, who got up and went downstairs. Shortly afterwards she heard the door bang and sounds of a scuffle taking place. She went downstairs and found her husband just inside the kitchen by the mangle, rolling about on the floor with blood streaming from his head and Eastwood standing over him with a hatchet in his hand. Eastwood took to his heels without uttering a word, as Clark's son, Jack, came downstairs and helped his mother carry his badly wounded father into the kitchen.

Eastwood immediately went from the Clark's house in Lister Road to Burgoyne Road Police Station, where he gave himself up. He said to Inspector Hughes, 'I want you to go to 20 Lister Road – I believe I have done Jack Clark in with a hatchet, which I have thrown away, probably in the chapel yard in Walkley Road.'

On Monday, 30 July, the same day Eastwood made his first appearance before Sheffield magistrates, the *Sheffield and*

*Rotherham Independent,* in their report of the murder under the headline BARMAN ATTACKED WITH A HATCHET, published an interview with Clark's eighteen-year-old-son, Jack. He told the reporters:

> I heard father go downstairs, and then I heard about six bangs, and I sprang out of bed and ran downstairs. My mother also ran downstairs, and I found her at the bottom of the stairs. Father was lying in the doorway huddled up in a heap against the mangle in the kitchen, with blood all round him, and blood spattered on the wall. He had some awful wounds on his head. Mother saw a man run round the passage with an axe in his hand. Father mumbled something as we carried him into the kitchen, and I ran to fetch Dr Exell, and found a police officer present on my return. They took father to the Royal Infirmary in the Fire Brigade ambulance, and he died soon after.

Newspapers also mentioned Mrs Ethel Eastwood's comments, when she was visited by reporters at the Bay Horse Inn, during Sunday. One report said a touching feature was Mrs Eastwood's deep concern for the dependents of her late employee. As she burst into tears she said, 'I am thinking of his wife and children, their breadwinner is gone.'

Reports went on to say that Mrs Eastwood had also announced her intention of visiting Mrs Clark. Throughout Sunday the inn remained opened and the bar was filled with customers discussing the terrible events of just a few hours earlier. The events had caused a sensation on the streets of Walkley and Hillsborough, where Eastwood and Clark were well known.

On the same day as the wider public of Sheffield were reading in the newspapers about the events in Walkley, in the early hours of the previous day, John William Eastwood was making his first appearance at Sheffield Police Court, before magistrates Mr J.C. Clegg and Mr R.G. Blake, charged with the wilful murder of John Joseph Clark. On the following day, the *Sheffield Telegraph* reported that:

> ... he maintained a cool and collected bearing. A heavily-built man, with bronzed and stern features, he was dressed

# BARMAN ATTACKED WITH A HATCHET.

## FOUND DYING AT KITCHEN DOOR.

### Early Morning Crime in Sheffield.

### SENSATIONAL SEQUEL.

### Ex-Publican Detained at Police Station.

A terrible tragedy occurred in a quiet street in the Walkley district of Sheffield early yesterday morning.

John Clark (48), stamper, of 20, Lister road, was found by his wife and son about 1.30 a.m. lying across the open doorway of the kitchen of his house in a pool of blood, with several severe wounds in his head.

He died at the Royal Infirmary at 4 a.m. following an operation.

A few minutes after the tragic discovery a man gave himself up to the police at Burgoyne road Police Station and made a statement, as a result of which he was detained, and will appear before the Sheffield magistrates to-day.

The man in custody is John William Eastwood (38), a chimney sweep and ex-licensee of the Bay Horse Inn, Daniel Hill street, where Clark was employed as potman and bar tender.

Eastwood and Clark were on terms of friendship and had, in fact, spoken to each other amicably only a few hours before Clark's death.

### HORRIFIED FAMILY.

A graphic story of the attack on his father was told to a representative of "The Sheffield Independent" by Mr. Jack Clark, 20-year-old son of the victim of the tragedy.

The family, comprising Mr. and Mrs. Clark, the two sons, Jack and Harry, and their grandfather, an old man of 74, were in bed when Jack was aroused by a knocking on the back door.

"I heard father go downstairs, and then I heard about six bangs, and I also ran downstairs, and I at the bottom of the stairs.

He was lying in the doorway, a heap against the mangle with blood all round him. He had wounds on his head, and wounds in his head.

... run round the ... hand.

... as I wa...

At the junction of Daniel Hill street and Harworth street, 14 months ago, Mr. Eastwood being the licensee.

The victim of the present tragedy was employed casually and for long spells, as barman at the inn, and his relations with both parties were most cordial and satisfactory.

Mr. and Mrs. Eastwood parted some little time ago, and Mrs. Eastwood refused admittance to her husband when he came back.

Following the estrangement the licence for the hotel was transferred to Mrs. Eastwood, the Sheffield justices assenting to the transfer only last Wednesday.

Since that time the husband has been to the Bay Horse many times as a customer, but his wife did not speak to him. On one or two occasions Eastwood is stated to have refused to leave the building at closing time, and the police were called to "persuade" him.

#### Friendly with Clark.

During all this time Eastwood and Clark met continuously, and were quite amiable to each other, and they chatted together at Saturday dinner-time.

On Saturday night Mrs. Eastwood stated her husband came to the inn, and he was quite sober, one of his drinks being a "lemon dash." He asked to

John Clark, the victim.

stay the night, and when this was refused he showed a strong disinclination to leave at closing time.

Eventually he left, reluctantly, after quite peaceful persuasion.

Mrs. Eastwood said she had a daughter, Ethel, aged 20, and a son, John William, aged 14.

Her husband, she said, was subject to morose fits. His father and uncle died in an asylum.

#### HATCHET FOUND.

#### MISSED FROM BACKYARD OF THE INN.

Mrs. Eastwood paid a glowing tribute to the character of the victim of the tragedy, and she had tried to effect a reconciliation between husband and wife, and ... back to Shef...

*A cutting from the* Sheffield and Rotherham Independent, *Monday, 30 July 1923, giving details of the events in Lister Road, in the early hours of the previous day, with a picture of the murder victim – John Clark.* (Sheffield and Rotherham Independent) in a blue suit, but was minus collar or tie. A hatchet, which it is said will play an important part in the case, was exhibited in court ...

During the proceedings Inspector Hughes said:

I ordered him [Eastwood] to be detained while I made enquiries ... On arriving at the house I found the back door closed, and the lights full on. I pushed at the door and it opened just a few inches. I then saw the naked foot of a man. I pushed the door forward and was able to get inside. There I found the unconscious body of a man who was lying full-length on his back with his feet towards the door. The man was only wearing trousers and a shirt. I examined the man and discovered two wounds on the back of his head. One was a very deep wound. Inside the house I saw the injured man's wife standing on the stairs. She said to me 'Jack Eastwood has done that; I don't know what he has done it for.' I sent for the ambulance and just afterwards the doctor arrived. A son of eighteen years had slipped away for him. In the meantime I had rendered first aid. Then the man was taken to the Royal Infirmary, where it was seen that he was too unconscious to allow for a deposition being taken. A consultation of the doctors was held and Clark was operated upon. At about 8.45 am the same morning the injured man passed away. At 10.30 am yesterday morning, after cautioning the prisoner, I charged him with the wilful murder of Clark. He replied, 'Yes, Sir.' On examining a chapel yard at the junction of Walkley Bank Road and Walkley Road, I discovered on the footpath about 500 or 600 yards from the deceased's man's home, the axe [produced in court]. There was fresh blood on it. I afterwards visited the Bay Horse Hotel [*sic*] in Daniel Hill Street, where the accused had been licensee up to a month ago, leaving on account of domestic trouble. The axe was identified as their property, and it was in the yard on Saturday evening.

Members of the public who had filled the courtroom to capacity were disappointed if they hoped to hear a dramatic story concerning any further details of the crime. The evidence given was very formal and on application of the police Eastwood was remanded until the following Saturday. An inquest was held on Tuesday, 31 July at the Coroner's Court in Nursery Street, before J. Kenyon Parker, Esquire.

The first witness was Eva Clark. She described how Eastwood had come to the house and what had occurred immediately after her husband had gone downstairs. The next witness to be called was Arthur John Hilton, who lived in Greaves Street. He said that Eastwood had been sleeping at his house for nearly a fortnight, 'in consequence of trouble at home'. Early on Sunday morning Eastwood called at Mr Hilton's house when he and his wife were in bed. He let himself in with a latch key and entered their bedroom. Mr Hilton said that Eastwood was sober, then added, 'I noticed the head and shaft of an axe in his trouser pocket; this struck me as unusual ... Eastwood said to me, "I am going to knock him up." He then chucked the key on the dressing table, saying, "I shall not require it any more ... Before he left the house I said to him, "Don't be a fool."'

Dr E.E. Clayton of the Royal Infirmary, who had conducted the post-mortem examination on Clark's body, provided the medical evidence. He said, 'Clark was admitted suffering from three wounds in the back of the head, two probably caused by the blunt side of some instrument. A gap had been caused in the skull that was 6 inches long, and 2½ inches wide, and the cause of death was the fracture.'

The next witness called was twenty-two-year-old Mildred Parramore. She was very emotional as she gave her evidence and said that she had known Eastwood for several months and that she had a conversation him on the morning of Saturday, 28 July, after she had bumped into him in Wallace Road, during the course of which Eastwood had said, 'If Ethel doesn't have me back, I'm going to do him in.'

Although Eastwood had not referred to John Clark by name, Mrs Parramore said she believed that was who he was talking about as he had said that kind of thing before.

Inspector Hughes was called next and repeated the evidence he had given at the Police Court the previous day. The last witness called was Constable Peach, who said following Eastwood's arrest, when he was taking him to the cells, he had told him, 'He let me in by the back door. As he was locking the door,

I hit him on the head with the hatchet. He fell to the floor, and then I hit him twice more.'

In his summing up, the coroner, in making reference to the police witness, pointed out that there was little doubt about the strict admissibility of certain statements, because they were made by a police officer who had not cautioned the prisoner making them. However, he added that as he had admitted them, they could not be ignored, being in the nature of voluntary admission, and not being extorted by any examination or questioning. He also pointed out to the jury that the question of sanity or insanity of the prisoner was not a matter for them to decide. The jury returned a verdict of 'wilful murder', which was received by Eastwood with his head bowed. As the coroner committed the prisoner to take his trial at Leeds Assizes, Eastwood was visibly shaking and his hands twitched uncontrollably. At the end of the proceedings, Eastwood was taken back to the Central Police Station.

On Friday, 3 August, a large crowd had gathered outside the deceased man's house in Lister Road to watch the funeral cortège leave for St Mary's Church, where a similar sized crowd had also gathered. Ethel Eastwood was one of the mourners. Following a short service John Clark's body was conveyed to the parochial cemetery nearby, where he was buried in the lower part of the cemetery. His wife Eva did not join him there until 1957. The grave they share there is unmarked.

On the following Saturday, Eastwood made a brief appearance at Sheffield Police Court, before Mr C. Whitehead and Mr W. Bush, when Detective Inspector Elliott asked that he be remanded until the following Friday. The remand was granted. After several further adjournments, Eastwood's committal proceedings were resumed on 21 August, when Mr J.E. Wing appeared for the prosecution and Eastwood was represented by the Sheffield solicitor Charles Wyril Nixon, who quickly showed that the basis of the defence was grounded in establishing Eastwood's insanity.

Under cross-examination Eva Clark was questioned about the relationship between Eastwood and her husband. She said that relations had been good and she knew of no reason why Eastwood would wish to hurt her husband. Inspector Hughes was asked information concerning Eastwood's background and family history, to which he replied, 'My enquiries show that he was admitted to the Eccleshall institution in February 1915 suffering from syphilis. His father and uncle both died in Wadsley Asylum, the former from paralysis, the latter from melancholia following war service.'

Dr Brockham of the Royal Infirmary, one of the doctors who had treated Clark, gave evidence about his injuries. Then, with reference to Eastwood, he was also asked about the link between syphilis, insanity and suicide. The packed courtroom heard Dr Brockham say:

> Many people with a history such as Eastwood had were mentally normal. Syphilis would not predispose a sufferer to suicide until he was quite off his head and if a man so suffering did go insane he did not recover.

William Weeks, who was walking out with Eastwood's daughter, said that not long after his return from Liverpool, Eastwood had, on 15 July, shown him a razor, and as he did so, said to him, 'This is for Jack Clark. He has told me to find somewhere else to sleep today. His wife objects to me sleeping on their couch and it means I shall be homeless. That's after promising me shelter.'

Weeks went on to say, when Eastwood brandished the razor again later in the day and reiterated his threat, he had taken it off him. He said during the fourteen months he had known him, Eastwood's conduct had always been queer. He had heard him threaten Mrs Eastwood on several occasions and he was always talking about doing the whole lot of them in. Such were Mrs Eastwood's concerns that her husband would harm someone that she had asked him to go and live at the Bay Horse Inn with them.

When Mildred Parramore was called she answered some of the questions put to her with no small degree of embarrassment, as unlike at the inquest, when the questions asked only served to determine how Clark had met his death, more probing questions about the background to the case obliged Mildred to reveal the facts of her infidelity. During the course of questioning, Mildred said that while they were in Liverpool Eastwood

had talked of killing himself. The remainder of the prosecution's case was based on evidence already heard at the inquest.
After all witnesses had been called, when asked if he had anything to say, Eastwood replied that he wished to reserve his
defence. The magistrates duly committed him for trial.

Eastwood's trial took place at the West Riding Assizes on
Friday, 7 December, at Leeds Town Hall, before Mr Justice
Talbot. Mr W.J. Waugh KC and Mr W. Hedley appeared for
the Crown, Mr F. J.O. Coddington, for the defence. The trial
lasted all day. In his opening speech Mr Waugh said:

> I submit that this is most deliberate, premeditated murder,
> that the prisoner knew what he had done, and that he gave
> himself up for that reason. The facts of the case are sordid,
> and there can be no doubt that the motive of the murder
> was jealousy. The prisoner was for a time licensee of the
> Bay Horse Inn, and Clark had acted at night as a barman.
> On the evidence to be given and on statement of the
> prisoner himself, there can be no doubt that Clark and the
> prisoner's wife were upon intimate terms. The prisoner left
> his wife on 30 June, and went away with a married woman
> named Parramore, for several days; then returned to
> Sheffield and quarrelled with his wife; next, for some days
> before Clark's death, the accused lodged with a man named
> Hilton in Greaves Street, Hillsborough. On the night of
> 28 July, Eastwood went into the bedroom where Hilton and
> his wife were sleeping, with an axe in his trousers pocket,
> and said, 'I'm going to knock him up.' He also threw his
> keys on the table and said, 'I shan't want them any more.'

Before Mr Waugh could continue one of the jurymen was taken
ill and collapsed in the box. Proceedings had to be halted while
a replacement juror, who also happened to be a man, was sworn
in. On resuming his speech, Mr Waugh said:

> Clark went from Hilton's to Lister Road, and Mrs Clark
> heard something rattling on a window and saw Eastwood
> outside. Her husband went downstairs to open the door,
> and just afterwards she heard a noise. Going downstairs,
> she saw her husband reeling in the doorway, and Eastwood

running away with a hatchet. Her husband was in a terrible condition, having three wounds on his head ... When the murdered man was examined by doctors it was found his case was hopeless ...

When Dr E.E. Clayton was called to give evidence there was no answer. Then his Lordship was told the doctor had sailed for China since the magisterial proceedings, and he was prompted to remark, 'It is extremely wrong to interfere with the course of justice in this way.'

The judge then imposed a fine of £50 on Dr Clayton, in his absence.

During the proceedings a large crowd had gathered outside the Town Hall to listen to the results of the city's candidates in the general election. Spasmodic bouts of loud cheering broke out as the results were announced, which contrasted widely with the events within the courtroom.

Police Constable Beresford said he received a complaint at the police station from Eastwood about Clark's attention to his wife. Eastwood said to the constable, 'It's a bit of a bugger if a man can't do as he likes in his own house. This man can come in when he likes, and if I can't, I will kill him.'

Police Constable Ellis said that he heard Eastwood say outside the police station, 'It's all over Clark and my wife. If I can't have her, Clark won't. I will kill him.'

In addition to the witnesses already heard at the inquest and the Police Court proceedings, the Crown called Dr R.D. Worsley, medical officer at Armley Gaol, and his assistant, Dr Hoyland Smith. Dr Worsley said in his opinion Eastwood was a sane man. During his period of observation he had seen nothing whatever to indicate that his mind was unhinged. While other medical evidence was being given concerning the state of the prisoner's health, Eastwood became extremely agitated and was clutching at his throat. Mr Coddington said that his client was feeling unwell. Eastwood was removed from the courtroom and when he returned after a few minutes had elapsed he looked much better. Sheffield police surgeon Dr G. Carter gave evidence concerning Eastwood's state of mind. During his evidence he remarked, 'I do not believe that more than one third of the people who commit suicide are insane.'

As the medical evidence continued the defence bided their time until an opportunity arose for them to attempt to influence the jury as to the state of mind of the prisoner. When it did, Mr Coddington interjected on the prisoner's behalf, submitting that he was insane at the time of the crime. Mr Coddington's interjection was fortuitous, because when Dr Hoyland Smith was called, his evidence appeared to add weight to the defence's claim regarding the prisoner's sanity. Contrary to what his colleague Dr Worsley had said regarding the prisoner's state of mind, Dr Hoyland Smith expressed the opinion that he considered Eastwood was not conscious of the gravity of the act he committed, but he probably realized an hour afterwards what he had done. During cross-examination of the medical witnesses, the defence had managed to include all the evidence at their disposal to highlight Eastwood's background concerning insanity in his family, as well as his own afflictions. In his closing speech Mr Coddington reiterated that his client was insane at the time he committed his crime, and stated that the accusation of misconduct against the wife was not proved. He invited the jury to return a verdict of 'guilty but insane'.

During His Lordship's summing up Eastwood became very restless and it was not long before he was taken ill again. His Lordship was able to continue with his summing up and the jury retired, giving Eastwood sufficient time to compose himself. They returned a little under three-quarters of an hour later to a hushed courtroom. Eastwood leaned on the dock rail to support himself as the foreman delivered the jury's verdict. They found the prisoner 'guilty', with a recommendation to 'mercy'. As soon as the verdict was announced Eastwood collapsed in the dock and had to be assisted to his feet.

When the Clerk of Arraigns asked if the prisoner had anything to say why sentence should not be passed, Eastwood replied, 'Whatever happened, I never meant to do it.'

After telling Eastwood that he had been convicted on evidence that had left the jury with no alternative but to bring in a verdict of guilty, Mr Justice Talbot donned his black cap and continued, 'You must not count upon the sentence not being executed, and I do earnestly beseech that you will use the short time which is yours to seek mercy where it can only be found.'

His Lordship then passed sentence of death upon the prisoner, following which Eastwood had to be carried from the dock in a state of collapse.

Eastwood's lawyers did not appeal against the conviction. A petition was organized in the hope of securing a reprieve; it contained more than 10,000 signatures. The date of Eastwood's execution was scheduled to take place at Armley Gaol on Friday, 28 December. On the day before the scheduled execution the Home Secretary announced that he could not grant Eastwood a reprieve and the law must take its course.

On Thursday night Eastwood was transferred from the condemned cell to a smaller cell nearer the scaffold. Although he passed what officials described as a 'fair night', when the time came on Friday morning to walk the few steps across the yard to the execution shed, it was necessary to assist him. In addition to the warders and prison doctor, those in attendance at the execution were the Sheriff of the County, Colonel F.R.T. Gascoigne, the Governor of Armley Gaol, Captain A.C. Scott, the acting Under-Sheriff, B. Dodsworth, Esquire, and the chaplain. The executioner was John Ellis.

At the inquest held later that morning before Leeds City Coroner, W.H. Clarke, Esquire, a verdict was returned that death was due to dislocation of the vertebrae caused by hanging of the neck, and properly carried out in accordance with sentence of death passed. Eastwood's body was subsequently buried within the precincts of Armley Gaol.

On Saturday, 29 December, the *Sheffield and Rotherham Independent* reported:

> Mr G.W. Gill, of 100 West Street, Sheffield, who organized the petition asking for a reprieve of Eastwood, visited the condemned man in his cell at Armley Gaol, Leeds, on Monday. To a representative of the *Sheffield and Rotherham Independent*, yesterday, Mr Gill said that Eastwood 'kept up his pecker like a man . . . He ate well and slept well, and said that he was happy to go. He was ready to die. He would be better dead than living under the conditions he had been for the last few months' . . . 'I could tell a lot,' said Mr Gill, 'but at present I cannot. Eastwood told me all about it, and who was behind it all; but I cannot say anything about that now

... He realized he had to die, and said that the sooner the end came the better.' Eastwood wished to thank everybody who signed the petition. He had no regrets, except that he was sorry for Mrs Clark, the widow of the victim.

The case of John Eastwood has two distinctions. This was the first capital case to be tried by Mr Justice Talbot (Sir George John Talbot, 1861–1938), who had only been appointed a judge earlier that year. John Eastwood was also the last person to be hanged by John Ellis (1874–1932), who hanged some high profile murderers during the early twentieth century, including Doctor Hawley Harvey Crippen, Frederick Seddon and George Joseph Smith (the 'Brides in the Bath' murderer). Ellis resigned in 1924. In the course of twenty-three years, he had executed 203 men and women. Later that year, Ellis tried to commit suicide. After drinking brandy heavily, he attempted to shoot himself through the head. He appeared before a magistrate, who told him, 'I'm sorry to see you here, Ellis. I have known you for a long time. If your aim was as true as some of the drops you have given, it would have been a bad job for you.' He was bound over to keep the peace for a year and to stay away from strong drink and thoughts of suicide. Ellis became very depressed in the years that followed. His health was not good and he continued to drink heavily. In September 1932, nine years after he had first attempted suicide, he slit his throat with a cut-throat razor. This time he did not bungle it. The coroner's verdict was 'suicide while of unsound mind'.

# Sources and Further Reading

### Chapter 1: Sheffield's Broad Canvas for Murder and Mayhem
*Sheffield Daily Telegraph*, 25 June 1879; 30 May 1881.
*Sheffield and Rotherham Independent*, 16 August 1802; 13 January,
    18 November 1868; 8, 10, 19, 26 March 1869; 3, 6, 14 June 1872;
    14 December 1876; 25 June 1879; 25 August 1890; 14 June 1892; 19 July
    1893.
*Barnsley Times*, 6 August 1859.

### Chapter 2: Murders in Sheffield 1782 to 1800
*Hull Advertiser*, 23 July 1796; 22 March 1800.
*Hull Packet*, 18 March 1800.
*Sheffield Iris*, 19 December 1799; 17 January 1800.
*Sheffield Local Register*, 7 March 1800.
*York Herald*, 15, 22 March 1800.

### Chapter 3: Murders in Sheffield during the Nineteenth Century
*The Times*, 16 June, 1, 12 August 1817; 30 March 1829; 4, 6 April 1835;
    17 July, 16 August 1837; 19 March 1842; 22 December 1852; 1, 10, 14,
    17 January 1853; 3 December 1875; 6 August 1884.
*Sheffield Independent*, 23 March 1822; 29 November 1828; 4 April 1829;
    8 April, 8, 22 July 1837; 24 December 1841; 19 March, 16 April 1842;
    22 August, 24 December 1852; 15 January 1853; 30 August, 1,
    4 September, 3, 22 December 1875; 12, 14, 15, 26, 29 July, 9, 27 August
    1884; 25, 26, 27, 29, 30 July, 6, 23 August 1887.
*Sheffield and Rotherham Independent*, 11 September, 24 December 1852; 1,
    15 January 1853.
*Sheffield Iris*, 10 June 1817; 28 March 1829.
*Sheffield Mercury*, 11 April 1835.
*Sheffield Telegraph*, 28, 30 August, 1 September, 3, 22 December 1875; 11,
    12 July, 6, 27 August 1884; 23 August 1887; 26, 27, 30 July, 6 August
    1887.
*Star*, 28 August, 2 December 1875.
*York Herald*, 2 August 1817; 9, 16, 30 March, 13 April 1822; 11 April 1835;
    12 August 1837.

### Chapter 4: Murders in Sheffield during the Twentieth Century
*The Times*, 2, 16 December 1913; 1, 19 August, 22 December 1925;
    22 October, 30 November 1927; 8, 9, 10, 14 August, 10, 11 October
    1945.
*Sheffield Independent*, 22, 23 October, 2 December 1913; 1 January 1914;
    22, 23 October, 2 December 1913; 1 January 1914; 28, 29 April, 19, 20,

21, 22, 26, 27, 28, 29, 30 May, 17, 18, 20 June, 29, 30, 31 July, 1, 17,
19 August, 1, 3, 8, 9 September, 2, 22, 25 December 1925; 1 January
1926; 22, 24, 27, 29 October, 3, 5, 30 November, 7, 21, 22 December
1927.
*Star*, 20, 22, 23, 28 October, 1 December 1913; 28, 30 April, 2, 6, 20, 21,
25, 27 May, 28, 29, 30, 31 July, 1, 18, 20 August, 1, 3, 4 September,
1 December 1925; 4, 29 November 1927; 7 January 1928; 9 August
1945; 10, 13, 24 March, 14, 22, 30 May, 10 June, 23 July, 14 August
1947.
*Sheffield Telegraph*, 22, 29 October, 2, 15 December 1913; 19, 26, 27,
29 May, 29, 30, 31 July, 17 August, 1, 3 September, 2 December 1925;
22 October, 3, 5 November, 21, 22 December 1927; 9 January 1928; 9,
10, 14 August 1945; 10, 12 March, 11 June, 22 July 1947.

### Chapter 5: Charles Peace and the Banner Cross Murder, 1879
*The Times*, 20 November 1878; 25 February 1879.
*Sheffield and Rotherham Independent*, 30 November, 1, 2, 4, 5, 6, 8, 9, 11,
12, 13 December 1876; 17, 18, 23, 29, 30 January, 1, 2, 5, 24, 25,
26 February, 5 July 1879.
*Illustrated Police News*, 1, 8, 15, 22 February, 8, 15, 29 March, 5 April 1879.
*The Trials of Edward Charles Peace*, Notable British Trials Series, Edited by
W.T. Shore, Wm Lodge, London, 1926.
*Murders and Murder Trials 1812–1912*, H.M. Walbrook, Constable, 1938.
*King of the Lags: The Story of Charles Peace*, David Ward, Elek Books, 1963.
*The Romantic Career of a Great Criminal*, N. Kynaston, Gaskell, London,
1906.

### Chapter 6: The Shelf Street Hatchet Murder, 1881
*Sheffield and Rotherham Independent*, 28, 29 30, 31 March, 1 April, 7, 10,
24 May 1881.
*Sheffield Daily Telegraph*, 28, 30 March, 7, 24 May 1881.
*Illustrated Police News*, 9 April 1881.

### Chapter 7: Murdered in a Caravan, 1889
*The Times*, 14 December 1889; 1 January 1890.
*Sheffield and Rotherham Independent*, 14 December 1889; 1 January 1890.
*Sheffield Daily Telegraph*, 19, 20, 22, 24 August, 14 December 1889;
1 January 1890.

### Chapter 8: The Woodhouse Murder, 1893
*Sheffield and Rotherham Independent*, 17, 18, 20, 21, 23, 25 February,
16 March, 1, 4, 5, 6, 7 April 1893.
*Sheffield Daily Telegraph*, 17, 20, 23, 25 February, 16 March, 4, 5 April 1893.

### Chapter 9: Murder at Christmas Time, 1905
*Sheffield Independent*, 26, 27, 29 December 1905; 5 January, 24 March,
11 April 1906.

*Sheffield Telegraph*, 26, 29 December 1905, 5 January, 24 March, 11 April 1906.
*Sheffield Star*, 26 December 1905; 4 January, 24, 27 March, 10 April 1906.
*The Times*, 28 March, 11 April 1906.

### Chapter 10: The Chinese Laundry Murder, 1922

*Sheffield and Rotherham Independent*, 18, 22 September, 2, 21 December 1922.
*Sheffield Daily Telegraph*, 23 September, 2 December 1922; 5, 6 January 1923.
*Star*, 16, 18, 19, 21, 22 September 1922.

### Chapter 11: The Walkley Murder, 1923

*The Times*, 31 July, 29 December 1923.
*Sheffield Daily Independent*, 30, 31 July, 4 August, 8, 28 December 1923.
*Sheffield Daily Telegraph*, 30, 31 July, 1, 6, 11 August, 8, 28, 29 December 1923.
*Sheffield Star*, 31 July, 6, 11, 22, 27 August, 7, 8, 28, 29 December 1923.

★  ★  ★

*Foul Deeds & Suspicious Deaths in SHEFFIELD*, Geoffrey Howse, Wharncliffe Books, Barnsley, 2009.
*Foul Deeds & Suspicious Deaths in SOUTH YORKSHIRE*, Geoffrey Howse, Wharncliffe Books, Barnsley, 2010.
*The Sheffield Hanged 1750–1864*, David Bentley, ALD Design & Print, Sheffield, 2002.
*The Sheffield Murders 1865–1965*, David Bentley, ALD Design & Print, Sheffield, 2003.
*The Sheffield Gang Wars*, J.P. Bean, D & D Publications, 1981.
*Sheffield Troublemakers*, David Price, Phillimore & Co Ltd, 2008.
*A History of Sheffield*, David Hay, Carnegie Publishing, 1998.

# Index